MW01097037

Charles Francis Haanel

THE
MASTER KEY SYSTEM
• CENTENARY EDITION •

Charles Francis Haanel

THE
MASTER KEY SYSTEM
• CENTENARY EDITION •

Live Your Life on Higher Planes

Published by JAH Holding, Inc.
Edited and annotated by Helmar Rudolph

THE MASTER KEY SYSTEM – CENTENARY EDITION
by Charles Francis Haanel

Originally published in 1912, 1916, 1919.

Published by JAH Holding, Inc.

Fourth Edition, June 2013
© 2010-2013, Helmar Rudolph – All rights reserved.
Design, layout, editing, and annotations: Helmar Rudolph

ISBN-10: 1456336045
ISBN-13: 978-1456336042

Website: www.MasterKeySystem.tv
Deutsch: www.MrMasterKey.com
Twitter: www.twitter.com/mrmasterkey
Facebook: www.facebook.com/mrmasterkey
Youtube: www.youtube.com/mrmasterkey

The contents of the Master Key System are placed in the public domain. The annotations are copyright Helmar Rudolph. You are welcome to use them, but please give proper credit and notify the author of any use of his intellectual property.

The typefaces used in this book are: "Yanone Kaffeesatz" by Dipl.-Designer Jan Gerner, "Vollkorn-Brotschrift" by Friedrich Althausen, and "Aller" by Dalton Maag Ltd.. The publisher is indebted to the outstanding work done by these typeface designers.

The whole range of the theory and practice of any system of metaphysics consists in knowing the Truth concerning yourself and the world in which you live; in knowing that in order to express harmony, you must think harmony; in order to express health you must think health; and in order to express abundance you must think abundance; to do this you must reverse the evidence of the senses.

The Master Key is based on absolute scientific truth and will unfold the possibilities that lie dormant in the individual, and teach how they may be brought into powerful action, to increase the person's effective capacity, bringing added energy, discernment, vigour and mental elasticity. The student who gains an understanding of the mental laws which are unfolded will come into the possession of an ability to secure results hitherto undreamed of, and which has rewards hardly to be expressed in words.

— CHARLES F. HAANEL

CONTENTS

INTRODUCTORY NOTES BY HELMAR RUDOLPH

Welcome, Namaste, In La'kech!

It was in February 2007 when I first came across Charles Haanel's Master Key System. I found it on Rhonda Byrne's website after watching her movie "The Secret" in Cape Town, South Africa, on a rainy winter's night some six months prior.

When I found a copy on Simon Templeton's Psitek.net website, saving and printing it was just a few clicks away. What followed suit in my own personal and professional life was nothing short of amazing. After many years of working at the junction of marketing consulting, database development and software innovation, I decided there and then to create the first ever German translation. Not even two years later, nearly 50.000 hardcover books were sold, a range of top quality audio products created, a forum and a study service, too, and talks given all over German-speaking Europe. It gave rise to five additional German translations, offering income opportunities to many a printer and publisher, and spreading Charles Haanel's wisdom even further.

Two more translations followed in 2009: "Ein Buch über Dich" and "Die erstaunlichen Geheimnisse der Yogis."

The "*Geheimnis des Lebens*" double-DVD of a talk I gave in Austria was released in March 2010, followed in December by "*Die Master Key Quintessenz*", a single-session alpha brainwave audio CD with the essence of the Master Key System. In March 2011 I released the "*Visual Master Key™*", where I placed almost 200 of the most important keywords from the Master Key System on a cylindrical, 360 degrees panorama for lateral thinking and accelerated learning. Mid-2011 I released the "*Ultimative Master Key*", a comprehensive commentary on the book. The children's book "*Sveta und die Macht des Meisterschlüssels*" was published in May 2012, accompanied by "*Cloudwalk*", a CD with the first ever musical representation of the journey through the Master Key System.

All those years, the vision of publishing an updated English version never left my mind, and this book is now the result. As 2012 marked the 100th anniversary of the Master Key System, I found it appropriate to add the tag line "*Centenary Edition*", indicating that it's something very special indeed. An humble undertaking for sure, but an important one nonetheless, as many find the form of speech and style of writing used by Charles Haanel outdated, and also may not relate to the old style of typesetting, never mind the antiquated image in which it is so often conveyed. Considering the time of its first initial publication, for many this may be a valid argument. It is for this very reason that I decided to publish this book.

Although I couldn't improve on Charles Haanel's deep insight and comprehensive understanding of the creative process, I did make a number of changes to the original:

- I chose a modern layout and typeface in an attempt to leave behind the dusty and in my eyes overused "this is some really, really secret stuff and therefore needs a sandy and dusty look" imagery, and present this wonderful gem of mental and verbal artistry in an appropriate manner.

- I added chapter titles.

- I added my own annotations to the existing copy, clarifying certain points and putting them into perspective.

- I highlighted in bold words, phrases or sentences that I deemed important.

- I added pictures and illustrations of the people mentioned, as an image conveys so much more than a mere word.

- Finally, I allowed myself to split some very long sentences into shorter segments, with the aim of making them easier to read and therefore understand. I can assure you that nothing of the original meaning has gone lost in the process.

- At the same time I published "The Master Key Brain Charger" as an accompanying checklist and premium workbook, which you can also purchase at www.masterkeysystem.tv.

Needless to say that the journey you are about to embark on will profoundly impact your own life and that of those you hold dear. It will profoundly impact the way you see things, the way you speak and act – in short, the way you live.

You are about to learn things that all of us should have, but neither did learn at school. Nor was the majority of us privy to this kind of ancient wisdom through the religious, cultural or social channels. Although all religious writings are replete with it, it's often put in analogies, parables or obscure language, or has even been falsified over the years.

In the Master Key System, which was initially published in form of a 24-week correspondence study course, author and businessman, doctor, psychologist, scientist and metaphysician, Charles Francis Haanel, explains to you the mechanism used for steering your life in any direction you desire. Every successful person uses this mechanism for their extraordinary results — some consciously, others unconsciously. Simply put, this mechanism is your ability to think the truth and subsequently express nothing but the truth.

It only deals with yourself, your innermost desires, discipline, and the determination to change your life to the better. It has nothing to do with a new religion, sect or organisational structure of any kind.

The Master Key System is a religion of One, and you yourself are the Guru. However, it should be noted that the kind of knowledge made public through this teaching was previously reserved for a select few, mainly because the vast majority wasn't capable of absorbing its wisdom. It therefore commands your respect and reverence.

It is like a chest of gold and a lottery jackpot at the same time. History has shown, however, that only a few can both handle vast riches or lottery wins. I sincerely wish for you that you belong to those few. It's your chance, ready for the taking!

The Master Key System deals with Natural Laws. It deals with Eternal Truth. Perhaps for the first time ever you are presented with a rational, scientific and logically conclusive explanation of the creative process and the operation of aforementioned laws.

You will learn how to control and relax both body and mind. You will learn the art of creative visualization, the art to create images in your mind and transform them down into tangible values. You will learn about the truth and how to convert it from an abstract concept into selfsame tangible values.

You will learn how to engage in deep concentration, in which you become one with the object of your desire, awakening and training your intuitive faculties and your drive for decisive action. Finally you will learn how to serve Mankind by having big ideas and making them real. All in all, the Master Key System provides you with a complete set of tools. How you use these tools is, however, entirely up to you.

Please do yourself the favour and refrain from reading it like a novel, tempting as it may be, for it is only through earnest study and the practical application of the exercises that you will come to enjoy the tremendous benefits this system holds.

The application of the Master Key will also interest communities, companies and organisations. If the combined mind-force of the multitude is directed towards a common and ethically correct goal, then socioeconomic miracles aren't only possible but inevitable. The same extends to rebalancing and harmonising our relationship with Mother Nature, least of all our own personal relationships.

With this vision in mind, I see my task in:

- Making this material available with my own annotations and comments.

- Offering you the best possible support through my website and other related channels.

Please be aware that the relatively few words contain a tremendous amount of meaning. This means that sentences are often deceptive as to the meaning they convey. There is just so much more to the content than first meets the eye, so take your time to read and re-read it as often as you can.

The application of the Master Key will enrich your life to an extent that is difficult to express in words.

- You will practice the power of conscious and systematic thinking and with it accomplish things that you previously didn't even dream of.

- You will become more attentive, clearer in your expression, and generally more goal-oriented.

- You will become more conscious and careful when choosing your words, for they are the result of your thinking and a precursor of your feelings and actions.

- You will become more sensitive and sensitive, more compassionate and understanding.

- You will become more intuitively intelligent and thus less dependent on your Conscious Mind.

- You will become motivated to see whatever you've begun through to fruition. It will make you sovereign in mind and decisive in action.

- You will attract new people and events into your life, and all of you will be enriched and blessed in the process.

- You will know the Truth, speak the Truth and live the Truth.

At the end of the day there will be a new »I«, with a new take on life and a never-ending source of power and inspiration, living in health, wealth and harmony. The circle is once again complete, and you have fulfilled your role as a conscious co-creator. Creation delights in you and rewards you abundantly for being in alignment with it.

Acknowledgements

I would like to thank and give credit to all those who made the image and contextual material available, in particular Wikipedia, Project Gutenberg, academic.ru, as well as the Tesla Society. Google. com and dict.cc were invaluable tools. Bible.cc and several other Bible sites provided additional content and insight. To all of you a heartfelt THANK YOU!

I would also like to thank John Sanders of New York, who's been on my toes for years, asking for a signed copy of the English edition. Well, John, the wait is finally over, and I hope you like what you see.

HELMAR RUDOLPH

Charles H. Haauel

CHARLES FRANCIS HAANEL BIOGRAPHY

Charles Francis Haanel was born in Ann Arbor, Michigan, on 22 May 1866 to parents of German origin. He began his business career in St. Louis, Missouri. He resigned his position in order to start his own company and eventually founded one of the largest conglomerates of his time, the Commercial Continental Company. He also had interests in other companies, before dedicating himself to writing and publishing.

Charles Haanel belonged to the American Scientific League, The Author's League of America, The American Society of Psychical Research, Pi Gamma Mu Fraternity, the St. Louis Humane Society and the St. Louis Chamber of Commerce.

He was awarded a Doctorate in Electronics (National Electronic Institute), Psychology (College of Divine Metaphysics) as well as Medicine (Universal College in Dupleix, India). His broad range of interests led him to author five books, which were published in St. Louis by Psychology Publishing and by his Master Key Institute in New York.

Charles Haanel put into books the ideas and methods he used to gain his success. Besides the »*Master Key System*«, which was first published in 1916, he also wrote »*Mental Chemistry*«, »*The New Psychology*«, »*A Book about You*« (1927) and, in collaboration with Victor S. Perera, »*The Amazing Secrets of the Yogi*« (1937).

Charles Haanel was Rosicrucian and speculative Mason in the 32nd degree (Sublime Prince of the Royal Secret) of the **AASR** (The Ancient and Accepted Scottish Rite), Keystone Lodge No. 243, A.F. & A.M. He entered the Eternal Lodge on 27 November 1949 and is buried in Bellefontaine Cemetery, St. Louis.

Walter B. Stevens described him as »a man of mature judgement, capable of taking a calm survey of life and correctly valuing its opportunities, its possibilities, its demands and obligations.«

Charles Haanel left us a legacy that we are only now coming to fully appreciate, but the time could not have been better suited. May his spirit live on in every single one of us applying the principles as laid out in the Master Key System.

INTRODUCTION

I

Before any environment, successful or otherwise, can be created, action of some kind is necessary, and before any action is possible, there must be thought of some kind, either conscious or unconscious; as thought is a product of Mind, it becomes evident that **Mind is the creative centre** from which all activities proceed.

It is not expected that any of the inherent laws which govern the modern business world as it is at present constituted can be suspended or repealed by any force on the same plane, but it is axiomatic that a higher law may overcome a lower one. Tree life causes the sap to ascend, not by repealing the law of gravity but by surmounting it.

ax·i·o·mat·ic – Adjective
Self-evident or unquestionable.

To control circumstances, a knowledge of certain **scientific principles** of mind-action is required. Such knowledge is a most valuable asset. It may be gained by degrees and put into practice as fast as learned. Power over circumstances is one of its fruits; health, harmony and prosperity are assets upon its balance sheet. It costs only the labour of harvesting its great resources.

The naturalist who spends much of his time in observing visible phenomena is constantly creating power in that portion of his brain set apart for observation. The result is that he becomes very much more expert and skilful in knowing what he sees, and grasping an infinite number of details at a glance, than does his unobserving friend. He has reached this facility by **exercise of his brain**. He deliberately chose to enlarge his brain power in the line of observation, so he deliberately exercised that special faculty, over and over, with increasing attention and concentration. Now we have the result a man learned in the lore of observation far above his fellows. Or, on the other hand, one can, by stolid inaction, allow the delicate brain matter to harden and ossify until his whole life is barren and fruitless.

Every thought tends to become a material thing. Our desires are seed thoughts that have a tendency to sprout and grow and blossom and bear fruit. We are sowing these seeds every day. What shall the harvest be? **Each of us today is the result of his**

A more modern example would be the mobile phone. Whereas after 1 minute you would be able to make a phone call, 2 minutes later you would know how to use it as a camera, 5 minutes as a music player, 10 minutes as an Internet device, so the more attention (time and thoughts) you pay to it, the more conscious you become of it, hence the higher the benefit you derive.

The greatest power of the mind requires that every conscious mental effort should involve a moral end.

past thinking. Later we shall be the result of what we are now thinking. We create our own character, personality and environment by the thought which we originate, or entertain. Thought seeks its own. The law of mental attraction is an exact parallel to the law of atomic affinity. Mental currents are as real as electric, magnetic or heat currents. We attract the currents with which we are in harmony—are we selecting those which will be conducive to our success? This is the important question.

Lines of least resistance are formed by the constant action of the mind. The activity of the brain reacts upon the particular faculty of the brain employed. The latent power of the mind is developed by constant exercise. Each form of its activity becomes more perfect by practice. Exercises for the development of the mind present a variety of motives for consideration. They involve the development of the perceptive faculties, the cultivation of the emotions, the quickening of the imagination, the symmetrical unfoldment of the intuitive faculty, which without being able to give a reason frequently impels or prohibits choice, and finally the power of the mind may be cultivated by the development of the moral character.

"The greatest man," said Seneca, "is he who chooses right with invincible determination." The greatest power of the mind, then, depends upon its exercise in moral channels, and therefore requires that **every conscious mental effort should involve a moral end**. A developed moral consciousness modifies consideration of motives and increases the force and continuity of actions; consequently, the well developed symmetrical character necessitates good physical, mental and moral health, and this combination creates initiative, power, resistless force, and necessarily success.

It will be found that Nature is constantly seeking to express harmony in all things, is for ever trying to bring about an harmonious adjustment for every discord, every wound, every difficulty;

15

therefore, when thought is harmonious, nature begins to create the material conditions, the possession of which is necessary in order to make up an harmonious environment.

When we understand that mind is the great creative power, what does not become possible? With Desire as the great creative energy, can we not see why Desire should be cultivated, controlled and directed in our lives and destinies? Men and women of strong mentality, who dominate those around them, and often those far removed from them, really **emanate currents charged with power** which, coming in contact with the minds of others, causes the desires of the latter to be in accord with the mind of the strong individuality. Great masters of men possess this power to a marked degree. Their influence is felt far and near, and they secure compliance with their wishes by making others "want" to act in accord with them. In this way men of strong Desire and Imagination may and do exert **powerful influence over the minds of others**, leading the latter in the way desired. The magnetic persons attract, allure and draw. They are emotional, and capture the will of others.

No man is ever created without the inherent power in himself to help himself. The personality that understands its own intellectual and moral power of conquest will certainly assert itself. It is this truth which an enfamined world craves today. The possibility of asserting a slumbering intellectual courage that clearly discerns, and a moral courage that grandly undertakes is open to all. There is a **divine potency in every human being**.

We speak of the Sun as "rising" and "setting," though we know that this is simply an appearance of motion. To our senses the Earth is apparently standing still, and yet we know it is revolving rapidly. We speak of a bell as a "sounding body," yet we know that all that the bell can do is to produce vibrations in the air. When these vibrations come at the rate of sixteen a second they cause a sound to be heard in the mind. It is possible for the mind to hear vibrations up to the rate of 38,000 a second. When the number increases beyond this all is silence again; so that we know that the sound is not in the bell; it is in our own mind.

The following paragraphs were later also used in Haanel's book, "*A Book about YOU*".

We can receive only what we give,
and we may give only to those who can receive.

We speak and even think of the Sun as "giving light," yet we know it is simply giving forth energy which produces vibrations in the ether at the rate of four hundred trillion a second, causing what are termed light waves, so that we know that what we call light is simply a mode of motion, and the only light that there is, is the sensation caused in the mind by the motion of these waves. When the number of vibrations increases, the light changes in colour, each change in colour being caused by shorter and more rapid vibrations, so that although we speak of the rose as being red, the grass as being green, or the sky as being blue, we know that these colours exist only in our minds, and are the sensation experienced by us as the result of the vibrations of light. When the vibrations are reduced below four hundred trillion a second, they no longer affect us as light but we experience the sensation of heat.

So we have come to know that **appearances exist for us only in our consciousness**. Even time and space become annihilated, time being only the experience of succession, there being no past or future except as a thought relation to the present. In the last analysis, therefore, we know that one principle governs and controls all there is. Every atom is for ever conserved; whatever is parted with must inevitably be received somewhere. It cannot perish and it only exists for use. It can go only where it is attracted, and therefore required. **We can receive only what we give, and we may give only to those who can receive;** and it remains with us to determine our rate of growth and the degree of harmony that we shall express.

The laws under which we live are designed solely for our advantage. These laws are immutable and we cannot escape from their operation. All the great eternal forces act in solemn silence, but it is in our power to place ourselves in harmony with them and thus express a life of comparative peace and happiness.

Difficulties, inharmonies, obstacles, indicate that we are either refusing to give up what we no longer need, or refusing to accept what we require. Growth is attained through an exchange of the old for the new, of the good for the better; it is a conditional or reciprocal action, for **each of us is a complete thought entity** and the completeness makes it possible for us to receive only as we give. We cannot obtain what we lack if we tenaciously cling to what we have.

The Principle of Attraction operates to bring to us only what may be to our advantage. We are able consciously to control our conditions as we come to sense the purpose of what we attract, and are able to extract from each experience only what we require for our further growth. Our ability to do this determines the degree of harmony or happiness we attain.

The ability to appropriate what we require for our growth continually increases as we reach higher planes and broader visions, and the greater our ability to know what we require, the more certain we shall be to discern its presence, to attract it and to absorb it. Nothing may reach us except what is necessary for our growth. **All conditions and experiences that come to us do so for our benefit**. Difficulties and obstacles will continue to come until we absorb their wisdom and gather from them the essentials of further growth. That we reap what we sow, is mathematically exact. We gain permanent strength exactly to the extent of the effort required to overcome our difficulties.

The inexorable requirements of growth demand that we exert the greatest degree of attraction for what is perfectly in accord with us. Our highest happiness will be best attained through our understanding of and conscious co-operation with natural laws.

Our mind-forces are often bound by the paralysing suggestions that come to us from the crude thinking of the race, and which are accepted and acted upon without question. Impressions of fear, of worry, of disability and of inferiority are given us daily. These are sufficient reasons in themselves why men achieve so little—why the lives of multitudes are so barren of results, when all the time there are possibilities within them which need only the liberating touch of appreciation and wholesome ambition to expand into real greatness.

Women, perhaps even more than men, have been subject to these conditions. This is true because of their finer susceptibilities making them more open to thought-vibrations from other minds, and because the flood of negative and repressive thoughts has been aimed more especially at them.

But it is being overcome. Florence Nightingale overcame it when she rose in the Crimea to heights of tender sympathy and executive ability before unknown among women. Clara Barton, the head of the Red Cross, overcame it when she wrought a similar work in the armies of the Union. Jenny Lind overcame it when she showed her ability to command enormous financial rewards while at the same time gratifying the passionate desire of her nature and reaching the front rank of her day in musical art. And there is a long list of women singers, philanthropists, writers and actresses who have proved themselves capable of reaching the greatest literary, dramatic, artistic and sociological achievement.

Women as well as men are beginning to do their own thinking. They have awakened to some conception of their possibilities. They demand that **if life holds any secrets, these shall be disclosed**. At no previous time has the influence and potency of thought received such careful and discriminating investigation. **While a few seers have grasped the great fact that mind is the universal substance, the basis of all things, never before has this vital truth penetrated the more general consciousness.** Many minds are now striving to give this wonderful truth definite utterance. Modern science has taught us that light and sound are simply different intensities of motion, and this may lead to discoveries of forces within man that could not have been conceived of until this revelation was made.

A new era has dawned, and now, standing in its light, man sees something of the vastness of the meaning of life—something of its grandeur. Within that life is the germ of infinite potencies. One feels convinced that man's possibility of attainment cannot be measured, that boundary lines to his onward march are unthinkable. Standing on this height he finds that he can draw new power to himself from the infinite energy of which he is a part.

II

Some men seem to attract success, power, wealth, attainment, with very little conscious effort; others conquer with great difficulty; still others fail altogether to reach their ambitions, desires and ideals. Why is this so? Why should some men realize their ambitions easily, others with difficulty, and still others not at all? The cause cannot be physical, else the most perfect men, physically, would be the most successful. The difference, therefore, must be **mental** – must be in the mind; hence mind must be the creative force, must constitute the sole difference between men. It is mind, therefore, which overcomes environment and every other obstacle in the path of men.

It is the actualizing of interior quality through the creative power of thought which has given us great leaders like Alexander, Napoleon, Cromwell, Marlborough and Washington; captains of industry like Carnegie, Morgan, Rockefeller and Leverhulme; inventors like Stephenson, Morse, Marconi, Edison, Tesla, and hosts of others. If, then, the only difference between men lies in their ability to think, to use and control their thought, to develop it—if the secret of all success, all power, all attainment is **the creative power of mind, the force of thought**—surely the ability of think correctly should become the paramount object of every man.

When the creative power of thought is fully understood, its effect will be seen to be marvellous. But such results cannot be secured without proper application, diligence, and concentration. The student will find that the laws governing in the mental and spiritual world are as fixed and infallible as in the material world. To secure the desired results, then, it is necessary to **know the law and to comply with it**. A proper compliance with the law will be found to produce the desired result with invariable exactitude. The student who learns that **power comes from within**, that he is weak only because he has depended on help from outside, and who unhesitatingly throws himself on his own thought, instantly rights himself, stands erect, assumes a dominant attitude, and works miracles.

Scientists tell us that we live in the universal **ether**. This is formless, of itself, but it is pliable, and forms about us, in us and around

It is because of their vision, discipline, continuity of purpose and unwavering confidence in the outcome.

Sol Luckman wrote in his book, "Conscious Healing": "The ancient Greeks were well aware of [torsion] energy, calling it "aether" and understanding that it is directly responsible for universal manifestation. In the 1950s Russian scientist Nicolai Kozyrev conclusively proved the existence of this life-giving subspace energy, demonstrating that, like time, it flows in a sacred geometric spiral resembling the involutions of a conch shell that has been called phi, the Golden Mean, and the Fibonacci sequence. In the face of overwhelming evidence of its existence, Western scientists are returning to the notion of aether using such phrases as "zero point energy" and "vacuum potential"... This breakthrough research in the temporal physics of subspace establishes that torsion energy permeates the entire multidimensional galaxy and not only is responsive to but may actually be consciousness creatively experiencing itself in time."

us, according to our thought and word. We set it into activity by that which we think. Then that which manifests to us objectively is that we have thought or said.

Thought is governed by law. The reason we have not manifested more faith is because of lack of understanding. We have not understood that everything works in exact accordance with definite law. The law of thought is as definite as the law of mathematics, or the law of chemistry, or the law of electricity, or the law of gravitation. When we begin to understand that happiness, health, success, prosperity and every other condition or environment are results, and that these results are created by **right thinking**, either consciously or unconsciously, we shall realize the importance of a working knowledge of the laws governing thought.

Those coming into a conscious realization of the power of thought find themselves in possession of **the best that life can give**; substantial things of a higher order become theirs, and these sublime realities are so constituted that they can be made tangible parts of daily personal life. They realize a world of higher power, and keep that power constantly working. This power is inexhaustible, limitless, and they are therefore carried forward from victory to victory. Obstacles that seem insurmountable are overcome. Enemies are changed to friends, conditions are overcome, elements transformed, fate is conquered.

The supply of good is inexhaustible, and the demand can be made along whatever lines we may desire. This is the mental law of demand and supply.

Our circumstances and environment are formed by our thoughts, We have, perhaps, been creating these conditions unconsciously. If they are unsatisfactory, the remedy is to consciously alter our mental attitude and see our circumstances adjust themselves to the new mental condition. There is nothing strange or supernatural about this; it is simply the Law of Being. The thoughts which take root in the mind will certainly produce fruit after their kind. The greatest schemer cannot "gather grapes of thorns, or figs of thistles." **To improve our conditions we must first improve ourselves**. Our thoughts and desires will be the first to show improvement.

To be in ignorance of the laws governing in the mental world is to be like a child playing with fire, or a man manipulating powerful chemicals without a knowledge of their nature and relations. This is universally true, because Mind is the one great cause which produces all conditions in the lives of men and women.

Admitting that you agree with everything that has been stated thus far, and most persons will take no exception to anything that has been said, it still remains to make a **practical application** of the law.

In order to take advantage of this law, and put ourselves into harmonious relationship with it, so that the benefit may be made manifest in our lives, it is necessary to see that the conditions are all met for its proper operation. We may know the laws governing electricity, we may have all the proper mechanism, the lamps, the wires, the switches, and we may even know how to generate the power, but if the connections are not properly made, we can work the switch till doomsday and no light will appear; so with **the Law of Attraction—it is in operation all the time**, everywhere, something is constantly being created, something is appearing, everything is continually changing, but to take advantage of this process, it is just as necessary to comply with the law as it is in the case of electricity or gravitation.

Mind is creative and operates through the Law of Attraction. We are not to try to influence any to do what we think they should do. Each individual has a right to choose for himself, but aside from this we would be operating under the law of force, which is destructive in its nature and just the opposite of the Law of Attraction. A little reflection will convince you that all of the great laws of nature operate in silence and that the underlying principle is the Law of Attraction. It is only destructive processes such as earthquakes and catastrophes, that employ force. Nothing good is ever accomplished in that way.

To be successful, attention must invariably be directed to the creative plane; it must never seek to deprive. You do not wish to take anything away from any one else, you want to create something for yourself, and what you want for yourself you are perfectly willing that everyone else should have.

You know that it is not necessary to take from one to give to another, but that **the supply for all is abundant**. Nature's storehouse of wealth is inexhaustible and if there seems to be a lack of supply anywhere it is only because the channels of distribution are as yet imperfect.

Abundance is a natural law of the universe. The evidence of this law is conclusive; we see it on every hand. Everywhere Nature is lavish—wasteful, extravagant. Nowhere is economy observed in any created thing. Profusion is manifested in everything. The millions and millions of trees and flowers and plants and animals and the vast scheme of reproduction where the process of creating and recreating is for ever going on, all indicates the lavishness with which Nature has made provision for man. That there is an abundance for everyone is evident, but that many seem to have been separated from this supply is also evident; they have not yet come into a realization of the Universality of all substance, and that mind is the active principle which starts causes in motion whereby we are related to the things we desire.

It is evident, therefore, that he who fails to fully investigate and take advantage of the wonderful progress which is being made in this last and greatest science, will soon be as far behind as the man who would refuse to acknowledge and accept the benefits which have accrued to mankind through an understanding of the laws of electricity.

Of course, mind creates negative conditions just as readily as favourable conditions, and when we consciously or unconsciously visualize every kind of lack, limitation and discord, we create these conditions; this is what many are unconsciously doing all the time.

This law as well as every other law is no respecter of persons, but is in constant operation and is relentlessly bringing to each individual exactly what he has created; in other words, »Whatsoever a man soweth that shall he also reap.«

Abundance, therefore, depends upon a recognition of the laws of Abundance, and the fact that Mind is not only the creator, but **the only creator of all there is**. Certainly nothing can be created, before we know that it can be created and then make the proper effort. There is no more Electricity in the world today than there was fifty years ago, but until someone recognized the law by which it could be made of service, we received no benefit; now that the law

Your reality is created in the Hypothalamus, which is part of your brain. It is there that all signals you receive through your senses are being interpreted. The "how" depends on the familiar, cultural, social and religious programming you have received over the years.

23

is understood, practically the whole world is lit by it. So with the law of Abundance; it is only those who recognize the law and place themselves in harmony with it, who share in its benefits.

A recognition of the law of abundance develops certain mental and moral qualities, among which are Courage, Loyalty, Tact, Sagacity, Individuality and Constructiveness. These are all modes of thought, and as all thought is creative, they manifest in objective conditions corresponding with the mental condition. This is necessarily true because the ability of the individual to think is his ability to act upon the Universal mind and bring it into manifestation, it is the process whereby **the individual becomes a channel for the differentiation of the Universal**. Every thought is a cause and every condition an effect.

This principle endows the individual with seemingly transcendental possibilities, among which is the mastery of conditions through the creation and recognition of opportunities. This creation of opportunity implies the existence or creation of the necessary qualities or talents which are thought forces and which result in a consciousness of power which future events cannot disturb. It is this organization of victory or success within the mind, this consciousness of power within which constitutes the responsive harmonious action whereby we are related to the objects and purposes which we seek. This is the Law of Attraction in action; this law being the common property of all, can be exercised by any one having sufficient knowledge of its operation.

Courage is that power of the mind which manifests in the love of mental conflict; it is a noble and lofty sentiment, it is equally fitted to command or obey. Both require courage. It often has a tendency to conceal itself. There are men and women, too, who apparently exist only to do what is pleasing to others, but when the time comes and the latent will is revealed, we find under the

Individuality glories more in the unfolding of the power within than in the servility of the weakling.

24

velvet glove an iron hand—and no mistake about it. True courage is cool, calm and collected, and is never foolhardy, quarrelsome, ill-natured or contentious.

Accumulation is the power to reserve and preserve a part of the supply which we are constantly receiving, so as to be in position to take advantage of the larger opportunities which will come as soon as we are ready for them. Has it not been said, "To him that hath shall be given." All successful business men have this quality well developed. James J. Hill, who recently died leaving an estate of over fifty-two million dollars, said: "If you want to know whether you are destined to be a success or a failure in life, you can easily find out. The test is simple and it is infallible: Are you able to save money? If not, drop out. You will lose. You may think not, but you will lose as sure as you live. The seed of success is not in you." This is very good so far as it goes, but any one who knows the biography of James J. Hill, knows that he acquired his fifty million dollars by following the exact methods we have given. In the first place, he started with nothing; he had to use his imagination to idealize the vast railroad which he projected across the western prairies. He then had to come into a recognition of the Law of Abundance in order to provide the ways and means for materializing it; unless he had followed out this programme he would never have had anything to save.

Accumulativeness acquires momentum; the more you accumulate the more you desire and the more you desire the more you accumulate, so that it is but a short time until the action and reaction acquire a momentum that cannot be stopped. It must, however, never be confounded with selfishness, miserliness or penuriousness; they are perversions and will make any true progress impossible.

Constructiveness is the creative instinct of the mind. It will be readily seen that every successful business man must be able to plan, develop or construct. In the business world it is usually referred to as **initiative**. It is not enough to go along in the beaten path. New ideas must be developed, new ways of doing things. It manifests in building, designing, planning, inventing, discovering, improving. It is a most valuable quality and must be constantly encouraged and developed. Every individual possesses it in some degree, because he is a centre of consciousness in that Infinite and Eternal Energy from which all things proceed.

Water manifests on three planes, as ice, as water and as steam; it is all the same compound, the only difference is the temperature, but no one would try to drive an engine with ice; convert it into steam and it easily takes up the load. So with your energy; if you want it to act on the creative plane, you will have to begin by melting the ice with the fire of imagination, and you will find that the stronger the fire, and the more ice you melt, the more powerful your thought will become, and the easier it will be for you to materialize your desire.

Sagacity is the ability to perceive and cooperate with Natural Law. True Sagacity avoids trickery and deceit as it would the leprosy; it is the product of that deep insight which enables one to penetrate into the heart of things and understand how to set causes in motion which will inevitably create successful conditions.

Tact is a very subtle and at the same time a very important factor in business success. It is very similar to **intuition**. To possess tact one must have a fine feeling, must instinctively know what to say or what to do. In order to be tactful one must possess sympathy and understanding, that understanding which is so rare, for all men see and hear and feel, but how desperately few "understand." **Tact enables one to foresee what is about to happen and calculate the result of actions.** Tact enables us to feel when we are in the presence of physical, mental and moral cleanliness, for these are today invariably demanded as the price of success.

Loyalty is one of the strongest links which bind men of strength and character. It is one which can never be broken with impunity. The man who would lose his right hand rather than betray a friend will never lack friends. The man who will stand in silent guard, until death, if need be, beside the shrine of confidence or friendship of those who have allowed him to enter will find himself linked with a current of cosmic power which will attract desirable conditions only. It is inconceivable that such a one should ever meet with lack of any kind.

Individuality is the power to unfold our own latent possibilities, to be a law unto ourselves, to be interested in the race rather than the goal. Strong men care nothing for the flock of imitators

Truth is the only solid ground in a world of conflict, doubt and danger.

who trot complacently behind them. They derive no satisfaction in the mere leading of large numbers, or the plaudits of the mob. This pleases only petty natures and inferior minds. Individuality glories more in the unfolding of the power within than in the servility of the weakling.

Individuality is a real power inherent in all and the development and consequent expression of this power enables one to assume the responsibility of directing his own footsteps rather than stampeding after some self-assertive bellwether.

Truth is the imperative condition of all wellbeing. To be sure, to know the truth and to stand confidently on it is a satisfaction beside which no other is comparable. Truth is the underlying verity, the condition precedent to every business or social relation. **Truth is the only solid ground in a world of conflict, doubt and danger**.

Every act not in harmony with Truth, whether through ignorance or design, cuts the ground from under our feet, leads to discord, inevitable loss, and confusion, for while the humblest mind can accurately foretell the result of ever correct action, the greatest, most profound and penetrating mind loses its way hopelessly and can form no conception of the results due to a departure from correct principles.

Those who establish within themselves the requisite elements of true success have established confidence, organized victory, and it only remains for them to take such steps from time to time as the newly-awakened thought force will direct, and herein rests the magical secret of all power.

Less than ten percent of our mental processes is conscious, the other ninety percent is subconscious and unconscious, so that he who would depend upon his conscious thought alone for results is less than ten percent efficient. Those who are accomplishing anything worth while are those who are enabled to take advantage of this greater storehouse of mental wealth. It is in the vast domain

This may explain the current state of affairs on Planet Earth. Whereas the vast majority is constantly focussing on material things which they perceive through their five senses – "the outer world" – only a select few are making conscious use of the power of their Subconscious Mind, their "inner world".

27

of the Subconscious Mind that great truths are hidden, and it is here that thought finds its creative power, its power to correlate with its object, to bring out of the unseen the seen.

Those familiar with the laws of Electricity understand the principle that electricity must always pass from a higher to a lower potentiality and can therefore make whatever application of the power they desire. Those not familiar with this law can effect nothing; and so with the law governing in the Mental World, those who understand that Mind penetrates all things, is omnipresent and is responsive to every demand, can make use of the law and can control conditions, circumstances and environment; **the uninformed cannot use it because they do not know it**.

The fruit of this knowledge is, as it were, **a gift of the Gods**; it is the "truth" that makes men free, not only free from every lack and limitation, but free from sorrow, worry and care. Is it not wonderful to realize that this law is no respecter of persons, that it makes no difference what your habit of thought may be the way has been prepared.

With the realization that this mental power controls and directs every other power which exists, that it can be cultivated and developed, that no limitation can be placed upon its activity, it will become apparent that it is the greatest fact in the world, the remedy for every ill, the solution for every difficulty, the gratification of every desire, in fact, that it is the Creator's magnificent provision for human emancipation.

III

The scientific spirit now dominates every field of effort, relations of cause and effect are no longer ignored.

The discovery of a region of law marked an epoch in human progress. It eliminated the element of uncertainty and caprice in men's lives and substituted law, reason and certitude.

Men now understand that for every result there is an adequate and definite cause, so that when a given result is desired, they **seek the condition** by which alone this result may be attained.

The basis upon which all law rests was discovered by inductive reasoning, which consists of comparing a number of separate instances with one another until the common factor which gives rise to them all is seen.

Inductive reasoning: to arrive at a generalisation of facts based on the commonalities shared by individual cases.

It is this method of study to which the civilized nations owe the greater part of their prosperity and the more valuable part of their knowledge. It has lengthened life, it has mitigated pain, it has spanned rivers, it has brightened the night with the splendour of day, extended the range of vision, accelerated motion, annihilated distance, facilitated intercourse, and enabled men to descend into the sea, and into the air. What wonder then that men soon endeavoured to extend the blessings of this system of study to their method of thinking, so that when it became plainly evident that **certain results followed a particular method of thinking** it only remained to classify these results.

This method is **scientific**, and it is the only method by which we shall be permitted to retain that degree of liberty and freedom which we have been accustomed to look upon as an inalienable right. The people are safe at home and in the world only if national preparedness mean such things as growing surplus of health, accumulated efficiency in public and private business of whatever sort, continuous advance in the science and art of acting together, and the increasingly dominant endeavour to make all of these and all other aspects of national development centre and revolve about **ascending life**, single and collective, for which science, art and ethics furnish guidance and controlling motives.

The Master Key is based on **absolute scientific truth** and will unfold the possibilities that lie dormant in the individual, and teach how they may be brought into powerful action, to increase the person's effective capacity, bringing added energy, discernment, vigour and mental elasticity. The student who gains an understanding of the mental laws which are unfolded will come into the possession of an ability to secure results hitherto undreamed of, and which has rewards hardly to be expressed in words.

It explains the correct use of both the receptive and active elements of the mental nature, and instructs the student in the

recognition of opportunity; it **strengthens the will** and reasoning powers, and teaches the cultivation and **best uses of imagination**, desire, the **emotions** and the **intuitional faculty**. It gives initiative, tenacity of purpose, wisdom of choice, intelligent sympathy and a thorough enjoyment of life on its higher planes.

The Master Key teaches the use of Mind Power, true Mind Power, not any of the substitutes and perversions; it has nothing to do with (Stage-) Hypnotism, Magic or any of the more or less fascinating deceptions by which many are led to think that something can be had for nothing.

The Master Key cultivates and develops the understanding which will enable you to **control the body** and thereby the health. It improves and strengthens the Memory. It **develops Insight**, the kind of Insight which is so rare, the kind which is the distinguishing characteristic of every successful business man; the kind which enables men to see the possibilities as well as the difficulties in every situation; the kind which enables men to discern opportunity close at hand, for thousands fail to see opportunities almost within their grasp while they are industriously working with situations which under no possibility can be made to realize any substantial return.

The Master Key develops Mental Power which means that others instinctively recognize that **you are a person of force**, of character – that they want to do what you want them to do; it means that **you attract men and things to you**; that you are what some people call »lucky«, that »things« come your way; that you have come into an understanding of the fundamental laws of Nature, and have put yourself in harmony with them; that you are in tune with Infinite; that **you understand the Law of Attraction**, the Natural laws of growth, and the Psychological laws on which all advantages in the social and business world rest.

Mental Power is creative power; it gives you the ability to create for yourself; it does not mean the ability to take something away from some one else. Nature never does things that way. Nature makes two blades of grass grow where one grew before, and Mind Power enables men to do the same thing.

The Master Key develops **insight** and **sagacity**, increased **independence**, the ability and disposition to be **helpful**; it destroys distrust, depression, fear, melancholia, and every form of

Note the emphasis on us emulating Nature in order to consciously create and therefore live a life in abundance.

The Master Key develops insight and sagacity, increased independence, the ability and disposition to be helpful.

lack limitation and weakness, including pain and disease; it awakens buried talents, supplies initiative, force, energy, vitality; it awakens an appreciation of the beautiful in Art, Literature and Science.

It has changed the lives of thousands of men and women, by substituting definite principles for uncertain and hazy methods – and principles for the foundation upon which every system of efficiency must rest.

The Master Key System is a practical wrapper for the 7 Hermetic Principles. You will find all seven principles being referred to and dealt with in this course.

Elbert Gary, the chairman of the *United States Steel Corporation*, said »The services of advisors, instructors, efficiency experts in successful management are indispensable to most business enterprises of magnitude, but I deem the recognition and adoption of right principles vastly more important.«

The Master Key teaches right **principles** and suggests methods for making a practical application of the principles; in that it differs from every other course of study. It teaches that **the only possible value which can attach to any principle is in its application**. Many read books, take home study courses, attend lectures all their lives without ever making any progress in demonstrating the value of the principles involved. The Master Key suggests **methods** by which the value of the principles taught may be demonstrated and put in actual practice in the daily experience.

Those methods consist of argumentation, visualization, and auto-suggestions.

There is a change in the thought of the world. This change is silently transpiring in our midst, and is more important than any which the world has undergone since the downfall of Paganism.

The present revolution in the opinions of all classes of men, the highest and most cultured of men as well as those of the labouring class, stands unparalleled in the history of the world.

Science has of late made such vast discoveries, has revealed such an infinity of resources, has unveiled such enormous possibilities and such unsuspected forces, that scientific men more and more hesitate to affirm certain theories as established and indubitable or to deny certain other theories as absurd or impossible. This way a new civilization is being born; customs, creeds, and cruelty are

31

This is not to be confused with what we usually call 'Ego'. We learn that there is only one consciousness, which expresses itself through the individual, including us. We learn to connect to those resources within the self by means of our own liberated mind and the application of correct and truthful principles.

passing; vision, faith and service are taking their place. The fetters of tradition are being melted off from humanity, and as the dross of materialism is being consumed, **thought is being liberated** and truth is rising full robed before an astonished multitude.

The whole world is on the eve of a new consciousness; a new power and a new consciousness; a new power and a new realization of the **resources within the self**. The last century (the 19th, Ed.) saw the most magnificent material progress in history. The present century will produce the greatest progress in mental and spiritual power.

Physical Science has resolved matter into molecules, molecules into atoms, atoms into energy, and it has remained for Sir Ambrose Fleming, in an address before the Royal Institution, to resolve this energy into mind. He says: »In its ultimate essence, energy may be incomprehensible by us except as an exhibition of the direct operation of that which we call Mind or Will.«

Let us see what are the most powerful forces in Nature. In the mineral world everything is solid and fixed. In the animal and vegetable kingdom it is in a state of flux, forever changing, always being created and recreated. In the atmosphere we find heat, light and energy. Each realm becomes finer and more spiritual as we pass from the visible to the invisible, from the coarse to the fine, from the low potentiality to high potentiality. When we reach the invisible we find energy in its purest and most volatile state.

And as the most powerful forces of Nature are the invisible forces, so we find that the most powerful forces of man are his invisible forces, his spiritual force, and the only way in which the spiritual force can manifest is through the process of thinking. **Thinking is the only activity which the spirit possesses**, and thought is the only product of thinking.

Addition and subtraction are therefore spiritual transactions; reasoning is a spiritual process; ideas are spiritual conceptions; questions are spiritual searchlights and logic, argument and philosophy is spiritual machinery.

Every thought brings into action certain physical tissue, parts of the brain, nerve or muscle. This produces an actual physical change in the construction of the tissue. Therefore it is only neces-

Neuroscience has long been able to measure brain activities, and has found that it makes no difference whether a person engages in an activity solely on a mental level or in real – the very same neurons are firing.

sary to have a certain number of thoughts on a given subject in order to bring about a complete change in the physical organization of a man.

This is the process by which failure is changed to success. **Thoughts of courage, power, inspiration, and harmony** are substituted for thoughts of failure, despair, lack, limitation and discord. As these thoughts take root, the physical tissue is changed and the individual sees life in a new light. Old things have actually passed away, all things have become new, he is born again, this time born of the spirit. Life has a new meaning for him, he is reconstructed and is filled with joy, confidence, hope, and energy. He sees **opportunities for success** to which he was heretofore blind. He **recognizes possibilities** which before had no meaning for him. The thoughts of success with which he has been impregnated are radiated to those around him, and they in turn help him onward and upward. He attracts to him new and successful associates, and this in turn changes his environment, so that by this simple exercise of thought, a man changes not only himself, but his environment, circumstances and conditions.

You will see, you must see, that we are at the dawn of a new day; that the possibilities are so wonderful, so fascinating, so limitless as to be almost bewildering. A century ago any man with an aeroplane or even a machine gun could have annihilated a whole army equipped with the implements of warfare then in use. So it is at present. Any Man with a knowledge of the possibilities contained in the Master Key has an inconceivable advantage over the multitude.

CHARLES F. HAANEL

Any Man with a knowledge of the possibilities contained in the Master Key has an inconceivable advantage over the multitude.

33

1

ONE CONSCIOUSNESS, ONE POWER

PART ONE

"Living the spirit" means creating those things in your mind, and allowing them to take hold, so that they turn into your "predominant mental attitude" by means of repetition – of exercise. It's not what you think every now and then what will manifest for you, but that which you have thought about so often, felt and acted upon that it has become habitual, then automatic, then subconscious. It is then no longer part of your conscious thinking. By means of your senses you will notice its fulfilment – this completes the feedback loop.

One of the Kahuna principles goes as follows: "Energy follows attention." Subsequently thoughts of loss will lead to more loss. How could it be any different?

It is my privilege to enclose herewith Part One of The Master Key System. Would you bring into your life more power? Then get the power consciousness. More health? Then get the health consciousness. More happiness? Then get the happiness consciousness. **Live the spirit of these things** until they become yours by right. It will then become impossible to keep them from you. The things of the world are fluid to a power within man by which he rules them.

You need not acquire this power. You already have it. But you want to understand it; you want to use it; you want to control it; you want to impregnate yourself with it, so that you can go forward and carry the world before you.

Day by day as you go on and on, as you gain momentum, as your inspiration deepens, as your plans crystallize, as you gain understanding, you will come to realize that this world is no dead pile of stones and timber, but that it is a living thing! It is made up of the beating hearts of humanity. It is a thing of life and beauty.

It is evident that it requires understanding to work with material of this description, but those who come into this understanding, are **inspired by a new light**, a new force, they gain confidence and greater power each day, they realize their hopes and their dreams come true, life has a deeper, fuller, clearer meaning than ever before.

And, now, Part One. . . .

ONE CONSCIOUSNESS, ONE POWER

1. That much gathers more is true on every plane of existence, and that loss leads to greater loss is equally true.
2. Mind is creative, and conditions, environment and all experiences in life are the result of our habitual or predominant mental attitude.
3. The attitude of mind necessarily depends upon what we think. Therefore, the secret of all power, all achievement and all possession depends upon our method of thinking.

36

4. This is true because we must »be« before we can »do,« and we can »do« only to the extent which we »are«, and what we »are« depends upon what we »think«.

5. We cannot express powers that we do not possess. The only way by which we may secure possession of power is to become conscious of power, and we can never become conscious of power until we learn that **all power is from within**.

Fortunately power is relative, not fixed. With the Master Key System you will learn how to increase your personal power, allowing you to accomplish bigger things and to fulfil your dreams with scientific accuracyh.

6. There is a world within; a world of thought and feeling and power; of light and life and beauty and, although invisible, its forces are mighty.

7. The world within is governed by mind. When we discover this world we shall find the solution for every problem, the cause for every effect; and since the world within is subject to our control, all laws of power and possession are also within our control.

8. The world without is **a reflection of the world within**. What appears without is what has been found within. In the world within may be found infinite Wisdom, infinite Power, infinite Supply of all that is necessary, waiting for unfolding, development and expression. If we recognize these potentialities in the world within they will take form in the world without.

9. Harmony in the world within will be reflected in the world without by harmonious conditions, agreeable surroundings, the best of everything. It is the foundation of health and a necessary essential to all greatness, all power, all attainment, all achievement and all success.

10. Harmony in the world within means the ability to control our thoughts, and to determine for ourselves how any experience is to affect us.

Controlling your thoughts means being aware of what is trying to enter your Conscious Mind. It is a constant exercise of vigilance, as most of what tries to gain entry is not your own and is rarely subjected a searching analysis.

11. Harmony in the world within results in optimism and affluence; **affluence within results in affluence without**.

12. The world without reflects the circumstances and the conditions of the consciousness within.

13. If we find wisdom in the world within, we shall have the understanding to discern the marvellous possibilities that are latent in this world within, and we shall be given the power to make these possibilities manifest in the world without.

37

14. As we become conscious of the wisdom in the world within, we **mentally take possession of this wisdom**, and by taking mental possession we come into actual possession of the power and wisdom necessary to bring into manifestation the essentials necessary for our most complete and harmonious development.

15. The world within is the practical world in which the men and women of power generate courage, hope, enthusiasm, confidence, trust and faith, by which they are given the fine intelligence to see the vision and the practical skill to make the vision real.

16. Life is an unfolding, not accretion. What comes to us in the world without is what we already possess in the world within.

17. All possession is based on consciousness. All gain is the result of an **accumulative consciousness**. All loss is the result of a scattering consciousness.

18. Mental efficiency is contingent upon harmony; discord means confusion; therefore, he who would acquire power must be in harmony with Natural Law.

19. We are related to the world without by the Subjective Mind. The brain is the organ of this mind and the cerebrospinal system of nerves puts us in conscious communication with every part of the body. This system of nerves responds to every sensation of light, heat, odour, sound and taste.

20. When this mind thinks correctly, when it **understands the truth**, when the thoughts sent through the cerebrospinal nervous system to the body are constructive, these sensations are pleasant, harmonious.

21. The result is that we build strength, vitality and all constructive forces into our body, but it is through this same Subjective Mind that all distress, sickness, lack, limitation and every form of discord and disharmony is admitted to our lives. It is therefore through the Subjective Mind, by wrong thinking, that we are related to all destructive forces.

22. We are related to the world within by the Subconscious Mind. The Solar Plexus is the organ of this mind; the sympathetic system of nerves presides over all subjective sensations, such as joy, fear, love, emotion, respiration, imagination and all

38

other subconscious phenomena. It is through the Subconscious that we are **connected with the Universal Mind** and brought into relation with the **infinite constructive forces** of the Universe.

23. It is the **coordination** of these two centres of our being, and **the understanding of their functions**, which is the **great secret of life**. With this knowledge we can bring the Objective and Subjective Minds into conscious cooperation and thus coordinate the Finite and the Infinite. **Our future is entirely within our own control**. It is not at the mercy of any capricious or uncertain external power.

24. All agree that there is but **one Principle** or Consciousness pervading the entire Universe, occupying all space, and being essentially the same in kind at every point of its presence. It is all powerful, all wisdom and always present. All thoughts and things are within Itself. It is All in All.

...which some of us call 'God', 'Allah', 'Brahma', 'Manitou', 'The Force', 'Zero Point Field', 'Infinite Intelligence' or 'Universal Consciousness'. It's a name for something that cannot really be named, for that would make it relative to something, which it cannot be. It is our feeble attempt to explain the unexplainable.

25. There is but one consciousness in the Universe able to think; and when it thinks, its thoughts become objective things to it. As this Consciousness is omnipresent, it must be present within every individual; each individual must be a manifestation of that **Omnipotent**, **Omniscient** and **Omnipresent** Consciousness.

26. As there is only one Consciousness in the Universe that is able to think it necessarily follows that your consciousness is identical with the Universal Consciousness, or, in other words, all mind is one mind. There is no dodging this conclusion.

27. The consciousness that focuses in your brain cells is the same consciousness which focuses in the brain cells of every other individual. Each individual is but **the individualization of the Universal**, the Cosmic Mind.

28. The Universal Mind is static or **potential energy**; it simply is; it can manifest **only** through the individual, and the individual can manifest **only** through the Universal. They are one.

29. The ability of the individual to think is his ability to act on the Universal and bring it into manifestation. Human consciousness consists only in the ability of man to think. Mind in itself is believed to be a subtle form of static energy, from which

It is absolutely essential that you control your thoughts so as to bring forth only desirable conditions.

arises the activities called "thought" , which is the dynamic phase of mind. Mind is static energy, **thought is dynamic energy** – the two phases of the same thing. Thought is therefore the vibratory force formed by converting static mind into dynamic mind.

All power, all wisdom, all presence is present within ourselves!

30. As the sum of all attributes are contained in the Universal Mind, which is Omnipotent, Omniscient and Omnipresent, these attributes must be present at all times in their potential form in every individual. Therefore, when the individual thinks, the thought is compelled by its nature to embody itself in an objectivity or condition which will correspond with its origin.

31. Every thought therefore is a cause and every condition an effect; for this reason it is absolutely essential that you **control your thoughts** so as to bring forth only desirable conditions.

32. All power is from within, and is absolutely under your control; it comes through exact knowledge and by the voluntary exercises of exact principles.

33. It should be plain that when you acquire a thorough understanding of this law, and are able to control your thought processes, you can apply it to any condition, in other words: you will have come into conscious cooperation with Omnipotent Law which is the fundamental basis of all things.

This conscious cooperation consists of your thinking the truth, and nothing but the truth, and subsequently expressing it in words, feelings and actions.

34. The Universal Mind is the **life principle** of every atom which is in existence; every atom is continually striving to manifest more life; **all are intelligent**, and all are seeking to carry out the purpose for which they were created.

35. A majority of mankind lives in the world without; few have found the world within, and yet it is the world within that makes the world without; it is therefore creative and everything which you find in your world without has been created by you in the world within.

36. This system will bring you into a realization of power which will be yours when you understand this relation between the world without and the world within. The world within is the **cause**, the world without the **effect**; to change the effect you must change the cause.

Remember the feedback loop!

37. You will at once see that this is a radically new and different idea; most men try to change effects by working with effects. They fail to see that this is simply changing one form of distress for another. To remove discord, we must remove the cause, and this cause can be found only in the world within.

This is particularly true for any kind of resistance. What you resist, persists!

38. All growth is from within. This is evident in all nature. Every plant, every animal, every human is a living testimony to this great law, and the error of the ages is in looking for strength or power from without.

39. The world within is the universal fountain of supply, and the world without is the outlet to the stream. Our ability to receive depends upon our recognition of this Universal Fountain, this Infinite Energy of which each individual is an outlet, and so is one with every other individual.

40. Recognition is a mental process. Mental action is therefore the interaction of the individual upon the Universal Mind. As the Universal Mind is the intelligence which pervades all space and animates all living things, this mental action and reaction is the **Law of Causation**. The principle of causation, however, does not obtain in the individual but in the Universal Mind. It is not an objective faculty but a subjective process, and the results are seen in an infinite variety of conditions and experiences.

You are only the channel of expression, not the originator, which is the Subconscious or Objective Mind.

41. In order to express life there must be mind; nothing can exist without mind. Everything which exists is some manifestation of this one basic substance from which and by which all things have been created and are continually being recreated.

42. We live in a fathomless sea of plastic mind substance. This substance is ever alive and active. It is sensitive to the highest degree. It takes form according to the mental demand. Thought forms the mould or matrix from which the substance expresses.

By "'practical understanding" Charles Haanel means converting the knowledge into day-to-day practice. Knowledge doesn't apply itself! Every day you need to apply it, and if you do, your life cannot but change accordingly.

These exercises are the aforementioned application - they are the system behind the Master Key. Failure to conduct them on a regular basis will result in no practical use or benefit, but in a mere mental satisfaction.

43. Remember that it is in the application alone that the value consists, and that a **practical understanding** of this law will substitute abundance for poverty, wisdom for ignorance, harmony for discord and freedom for tyranny, and certainly there can be no greater blessing than these from a material and social standpoint.

44. Now make the application: Select a room where you can be alone and undisturbed; sit erect, comfortably, but do not lounge; let your thoughts roam where they will but be perfectly still for from fifteen minutes to half an hour; continue this for three or four days or for a week until you secure full control of your physical being.

45. Many will find this extremely difficult; others will conquer with ease, but it is absolutely essential to secure complete control of the body before you are ready to progress. Next week you will receive instructions for the next step; in the meantime you must have mastered this one.

"Nurture your mind with great thoughts; to believe in the heroic makes heroes."
— BENJAMIN DISRAELI

42

PART ONE — QUESTIONS AND ANSWERS

1. *What is the world without in its relation to the world within?*
   The world without is a reflection of the world within.

2. *Upon what does all possession depend?*
   All possession is based on consciousness.

3. *How is the individual related to the objective world?*
   The individual is related to the objective world by the Subjective Mind. The brain is the organ of this mind.

4. *How is he related to the Universal Mind?*
   He is related to the Universal Mind by the Subconscious Mind; the Solar Plexus is the organ of this mind.

5. *What is the Universal Mind?*
   The Universal Mind is the life principle of every atom which is in existence.

6. *How can the Individual act on the Universal?*
   The ability of the individual to think is his ability to act upon the Universal and bring it into manifestation.

7. *What is the result of this action and interaction?*
   The result of this action and interaction is cause and effect; every thought is a cause and every condition an effect.

8. *How are harmonious and desirable conditions secured?*
   Harmonious and desirable conditions are obtained by right thinking.

9. *What is the cause of all discord, inharmony, lack and limitation?*
   Discord, inharmony, lack and limitation are the result of wrong thinking.

10. *What is the source of all powers?*
    The source of all power is the world within, the Universal Fountain of Supply, the Infinite Energy of which each individual is an outlet.

2

ONE METHOD OF FINDING THE TRUTH

Our difficulties are largely due to confused ideas and ignorance of our true interests. The great task is to **discover the laws of nature** to which we are to adjust ourselves. **Clear thinking and moral insight** are, therefore, of incalculable value. All processes, even those of thought, rest on solid foundations.

The keener the sensibilities, the more acute the judgment, the more delicate the taste, the more refined the moral feelings, the more subtle the intelligence, the loftier the aspiration, the purer and more intense are the gratifications which existence yields. Hence it is that the study of the best that has been thought in the world gives supreme pleasure.

The powers, uses and possibilities of the mind under the new interpretations are incomparably more wonderful that the most extravagant accomplishment, or even dreams of material progress. Thought is energy. Active thought is active energy; concentrated thought is concentrated energy. **Thought concentrated on a definite purpose becomes power.** This is the power which is being used by those who do not believe in the virtue of poverty, or the beauty of self-denial. They perceive that this is the talk of weaklings.

The ability to receive and manifest this power depends upon the ability to recognize the Infinite Energy ever dwelling in man, constantly creating and recreating his body and mind, and ready at any moment to manifest through him in any needful manner. In **exact proportion** to the recognition of this truth will be the manifestation in the outer life of the individual.

Part Two explains the method by which this is accomplished.

What goes in, must come out! In a vibratory universe, thoughts correspond to like thoughts. Proof of it can also be seen in the harmonic resonance of the musical scale.

ONE METHOD OF FINDING THE TRUTH

I. The operations of the mind are produced by two parallel modes of activity, the one conscious, and the other subconscious. Professor Davidson says: »He who thinks to illuminate the whole range of mental action by the light of his own consciousness is not unlike the one who should go about to illuminate the Universe with a rushlight.«

46

2. The Subconscious' logical processes are carried on with a certainty and regularity which would be impossible if there existed the possibility of error. Our mind is so designed that it prepares for us the most important foundations of cognition, whilst we have **not the slightest apprehension of the modus operandi**.

3. The subconscious soul, like a benevolent stranger, works and makes provision for our benefit, pouring only the mature fruit into our lap. Thus, the ultimate analysis of thought processes shows that the Subconscious is the theatre of the most important mental phenomena.

4. It is through the Subconscious that Shakespeare must have perceived, without effort, great truths which are hidden from the Conscious Mind of the student; that Phidias fashioned marble and bronze; that Raphael painted Madonnas and Beethoven composed symphonies.

5. Ease and perfection depend entirely upon the degree in which we **cease to depend upon the consciousness**; playing the piano, skating, operating the typewriter, the skilled trades, depend for their perfect execution on the process of the Subconscious Mind. The marvel of playing a brilliant piece on the piano, while at the same time conducting a vigorous conversation, shows the greatness of our subconscious powers.

6. We are all aware how dependent we are upon the Subconscious, and the greater, the nobler, the more brilliant our thoughts are, the more it is obvious to ourselves that the origin lies beyond our ken. We find ourselves endowed with tact, instinct, sense of the beautiful in art, music, etc., of whose origin or dwelling place we are wholly unconscious.

7. The value of the Subconscious is enormous; it inspires us; it warns us; it furnishes us with names, facts and scenes from the storehouse of memory. It directs our thoughts, tastes, and accomplishes tasks so intricate that no Conscious Mind, even if it had the power, has the capacity for.

8. We can walk at will; we can raise the arm whenever we choose to do so; we can give our attention through eye or ear to any subject at pleasure. On the other hand, we cannot stop our

As you carry on with your studies you will learn how to increasingly depend on your intuitive powers – your 'gut feel', and less on your reasoning will.

47

heartbeats nor the circulation of the blood, nor the growth of stature, nor the formation of nerve and muscle tissue, nor the building of the bones, nor many other important vital processes.

9. If we compare these two sets of action, the one decreed by the will of the moment, and the other proceeding in majestic, rhythmic course, subject to no vacillation, but constant at every moment, we stand in awe of the latter, and ask to have the mystery explained. We see at once that these are the vital processes of our physical life, and we cannot avoid the inference that these all-important functions are **designedly withdrawn from the domain of our outward will** with its variations and transitions, and placed under the direction of **a permanent and dependable power within us**.

This power within us is permanent and dependable! Understanding this permanently removes fear, worry, anxiety and doubt.

10. Of these two powers, the outward and changeable has been termed the »Conscious Mind,« or the »Objective Mind« (dealing with outward objects). The interior power is called the »Subconscious Mind,« or the »Subjective Mind,« and besides its work on the mental plane it controls the regular functions which make physical life possible.

11. It is necessary to have a clear understanding of their respective functions on the mental plane, as well as of certain other basic principles. Perceiving and operating through the five physical senses, **the Conscious Mind deals with the impressions and objects of the outward life**.

Inductive: from the specific to the generic; comparing individual cases in order to find the common denominator, to be able to make general statements.

Deductive: from the generic to the specific.

Analytical: implicit understanding, i.e. "All bachelors are unmarried."

Syllogistic: a type of logical arguments, i.e. "All men are mortal. All Greeks are men. Therefore all Greeks are mortal."

12. It has the faculty of discrimination, carrying with it the responsibility of choice. It has the power of reasoning – whether inductive, deductive, analytical or syllogistic – and this power may be developed to a high degree. It is the seat of the will with all the energies that flow therefrom.

13. Not only can it impress other minds, but it can direct the Subconscious Mind. In this way the Conscious Mind becomes the responsible ruler and guardian of the Subconscious Mind. It is this high function which can completely reverse conditions in your life.

14. It is often true that conditions of fear, worry, poverty, disease, inharmony and evils of all kinds dominate us **by reason of false suggestions** accepted by the unguarded

Subconscious Mind. All this the trained Conscious Mind can entirely prevent by its vigilant protective action. It may properly be called »the watchman at the gate« of the great subconscious domain.

15. One writer has expressed the chief distinction between the two phases of mind thus: »Conscious Mind is reasoning will. Subconscious Mind is instinctive desire, the result of past reasoning will.«

16. The Subconscious Mind draws just and accurate inferences from premises furnished from outside sources. Where the premise is true, the Subconscious Mind reaches a faultless conclusion, but, where the premise or suggestion is an error, the whole structure falls. **The Subconscious Mind does not engage in the process of proving**. It relies upon the Conscious Mind, »the watchman at the gate«, to guard it from mistaken impressions.

Only Truth will prevail. Any kind of error is by definition doomed to failure as it lacks principle, but it will first create havoc on the mental, emotional and physical plane.

17. Receiving any suggestions as true, the Subconscious Mind at once proceeds to act thereon in the whole domain of its tremendous field of work. The Conscious Mind can suggest either truth or error. If the latter, it is at the cost of wide-reaching peril to the whole being.

18. The Conscious Mind ought to be on duty during every waking hour. When the »watchman« is »off guard«, or when its calm judgment is suspended, under a variety of circumstances, then the Subconscious Mind is unguarded and left open to suggestion from all sources. During the wild excitement of panic, or during the height of anger, or the impulses of the irresponsible mob, or at any other time of unrestrained passion, the conditions are most dangerous. The Subconscious Mind is then open to the suggestion of fear, hatred, selfishness, greed, self- depreciation and other negative forces, derived from surrounding persons or circumstances. The result is usually unwholesome in the extreme, with effects that may endure to distress it for a long time. Hence, the great importance of guarding the Subconscious Mind from false impressions.

Are you taking any kind of depressants or stimulants? If yes, you may want to think this over in light of this newly obtained information.

This is why the Master Key System leads you towards strengthening your intuitive powers, so that you can take full advantage of the faultless operation of the Subconscious Mind.

Those who have a harmonious mental attitude will find this reflected in their normal dealings in life, including business matters like interviews or difficult decisions.

This is a safeguard, because otherwise everything you think would immediately become real for you, resulting in total chaos due to your untrained mind.

This is a great help, as freedom implies an unrestricted flow of energy and therefore order, harmony, beauty, love, and therefore the continuation of any kind of life.

19. **The Subconscious Mind perceives by intuition**. Hence, its processes are rapid. It does not wait for the slow methods of conscious reasoning. In fact, it can not employ them.

20. The Subconscious Mind never sleeps, never rests, any more than does your heart, or your blood. It has been found that by plainly stating to the Subconscious Mind certain specific things to be accomplished, forces are set in operation that lead to the result desired. Here, then, is **a source of power which places us in touch with Omnipotence**. Here in is a deep principle which is well worth our most earnest study.

21. The operation of this law is interesting. Those who put it into operation find that when they go out to meet the person with whom they anticipate a difficult interview, something has been there before them and dissolved the supposed differences; everything is changed; all is harmonious. They find that when some difficult business problem presents itself they can afford to make delay and something suggests the proper solution; everything is properly arranged. In fact, those who have learned to trust the Subconscious find that they have infinite resources at their command.

22. The Subconscious Mind is the seat of our principles and our aspirations. It is the fount of our artistic and altruistic ideals. These instincts can only be overthrown by an **elaborate and gradual process of undermining** the innate principles.

23. The Subconscious Mind **cannot** argue controversially. Hence, if it has accepted wrong suggestions, the sure method of overcoming them is by the use of **a strong counter suggestion, frequently repeated**, which the Subconscious Mind **must t**, thus eventually forming new and healthy habits of thought and life, for the Subconscious Mind is the seat of Habit. That which we do over and over becomes mechanical; it is no longer an act of judgment, but has worn its deep grooves in the Subconscious Mind. This is favourable for us if the habit be wholesome and right. If it be harmful, and wrong, the remedy is to recognize the omnipotence of the Subconscious Mind and suggest **present actual freedom**. The Subconscious being creative and one with our divine source will at once create the freedom suggested.

The sure method of overcoming wrong suggestions is by the use of a strong counter suggestion, often repeated, which the Subconscious Mind must accept.

24. To sum up: The normal functions of the Subconscious on the physical side have to do with the regular and vital processes, with the preservation of life and the restoration of health; with the care of offspring, which includes an instinctive desire to **preserve all life** and improve conditions generally.

25. On the mental side, it is the storehouse of memory; it harbours the wonderful thought messengers, who work, **unhampered by time or space**; it is the fountain of the practical initiative and constructive forces of life: It is the seat of habit.

26. On the spiritual side, it is the source of ideals, of aspiration, of the imagination, and is the channel through which we recognize our Divine Source, and in proportion as we recognize this divinity do we come into an understanding of the source of power.

27. Some one may ask: »How can the Subconscious change conditions?« The reply is, because the Subconscious is a part of the Universal Mind and a part must be the same in kind and quality as the whole; the only difference is one of degree. The whole, as we know, is creative, in fact, it is the only creator there is, consequently, we find that mind is creative, and as thought is the only activity which the mind possesses thought must necessarily be creative also.

28. But we shall find that there is a vast difference between simply thinking, and directing our thought **consciously, systematically and constructively**; when we do this we place our mind in harmony with the Universal Mind, we come in tune with the Infinite, we set in operation the mightiest force in existence, the creative power of the Universal Mind. This, as everything else, is governed by natural law, and this law is the »Law of Attraction,« which is that mind is creative, and

Be sure to re-read this section until you have grasped its full meaning and significance.

51

will automatically correlate with its object and bring it into manifestation.

29. Last week I gave you an exercise for the purpose of securing control of the physical body; if you have accomplished this you are ready to advance. This time you will begin to control your thought. Always take the same room, the same chair, and the same position, if possible. In some cases it is not convenient to take the same room, in this case simply make the best use of such conditions as may be available. Now be perfectly still as before, but inhibit all thought; this will give you control over all thoughts of care, worry and fear, and will enable you to entertain only the kind of thoughts you desire. Continue this exercise until you gain **complete mastery**.

30. You will not be able to do this for more that a few moments at a time, but the exercise is valuable, because it will be a very practical demonstration of the great number of thoughts which are constantly trying to gain access to your mental world.

31. Next week you will receive instructions for an exercise which may be a little more interesting, but **it is necessary that you master this one first**.

Physical control is followed by mental control. You can only control yourself mentally when you can control yourself physically. All the exercises of the first half are building on top of each other. They are the foundation for the remainder of the exercies, so please ensure that you master each one of them.

> *"Cause and effect is as absolute and unde-*
> *viating in the hidden realm of thought*
> *as in the world of visible and material*
> *things. Mind is the master weaver, both*
> *of the interior garment of character and*
> *the outer garment of circumstance."*
> — JAMES ALLEN

11. *What are the two modes of mental activity?*
Conscious and subconscious.

12. *Upon what do ease and perfection depend?*
Ease and perfection depend entirely upon the degree in
which we cease to depend upon the Conscious Mind.

13. *What is the value of the Subconscious?*
It is enormous; it guides us, warns us, it controls
the vital processes and is the seat of memory.

14. *What are some of the functions of the Conscious Mind?*
It has the faculty of discrimination; it has
the power of reasoning; it is the seat of the
will and may impress the Subconscious.

15. *How has the distinction between the Conscious
and Subconscious been expressed?*
»Conscious Mind is reasoning will. Subconscious Mind
is instinctive desire, the result of past reasoning will.«

16. *What method is necessary in order to
impress the Subconscious?*
Mentally state what is wanted.

17. *What will be the result?*
If the desire is in harmony with the forward
movement of the Great Whole, forces will be set
in motion which will bring about the result.

18. *What is the result of the operation of this law?*
Our environment reflects conditions corresponding to
the predominant mental attitude which we entertain.

19. *What names has been given to this law?*
The Law of Attraction.

20. *How is the law stated?*
Thought is a creative energy, and will automatically
correlate with is object and bring it into manifestation.

53

3

THOUGHTS BECOME THINGS

You have found that the Individual may act on the Universal, and that the result of this action and interaction is cause and effect. Thought, therefore, is the cause, and the experiences with which you meet in life are the effect.

Eliminate, therefore, any possible tendency to complain of conditions as they have been, or as they are, because it rests with you to change them and make them what you would like them to be.

Direct your effort to a realization of the mental resources, always at your command, from which all real and lasting power comes.

Persist in this practice until you come to a realization of the fact that there can be no failure in the accomplishment of any proper object in life if you but understand your power and persist in your object, because the mind-forces are **ever ready to lend themselves to a purposeful will**, in the effort to crystallize thought and desire into actions, events and conditions.

Whereas in the beginning of each function of life and each action is the result of conscious thought, the habitual actions become automatic and the thought that controls them passes into the realm of the Subconscious; yet it is just as intelligent as before. It is necessary that it become automatic, or subconscious, in order that the self-Conscious Mind may attend to other things. The new actions will, however, in their turn, become habitual, then automatic, then subconscious in order that the mind again may be freed from this detail and advanced to still other activities.

When you realize this, you will have found **a source of power** which will enable you to take care of any situation in life which may develop.

THOUGHTS BECOME THINGS

I. The necessary interaction of the Conscious and Subconscious Mind requires **a similar interaction between the corresponding systems of nerves**. Judge Troward indicates the very beautiful method in which this interaction is effected. He says: The cerebrospinal system is the organ of the Conscious Mind and the sympathetic is the organ of the Subconscious.

It's like walking, eating or driving a car. Whereas initially it required all your attention, through repetition it has become automatic and thus subconscious. You no longer think about it – it just happens; you just 'do it'.

56

The cerebrospinal is the channel through which we receive conscious perception from the physical senses and exercise control over the movements of the body. This system of nerves has its centre in the brain.

2. The Sympathetic System has its centre in a ganglionic mass at the back of the stomach known as the **Solar Plexus** (left), and is the channel of that mental action which unconsciously supports the vital functions of the body.

3. The connection between the two systems is made by the **Vagus nerve** (right) which passes out of the cerebral region as a portion of the voluntary system to the thorax, sending out branches to the heart and lungs, and finally passing through the diaphragm, where it loses its outer coating and becomes identified with the nerves of the Sympathetic System, so forming a connecting link between the two and making man physically a »single entity«.

4. We have seen that every thought is received by the brain, which is the organ of the Conscious; it is here subjected to our power of reasoning. When the Objective Mind has been satisfied that the thought is true, it is sent to the Solar Plexus, or the brain of the Subjective Mind, to be made into our flesh, to be brought forth into the world as reality. It is then no longer susceptible to any argument whatsoever. **The Subconscious Mind cannot argue; it only acts**. It accepts the conclusions of the Objective Mind as final.

5. The Solar Plexus has been likened to the Sun of the body, because it is a **central point of distribution** for the energy which the body is constantly generating. This energy is very real energy, and this Sun is a very real Sun, and the energy is being distributed by very real nerves to all parts of the body, and is thrown off in an atmosphere which envelopes the body.

6. If this radiation is sufficiently strong the person is called magnetic; he is said to be filled with **personal magnetism**. Such a person may wield an immense power for good. His presence alone will often bring comfort to the troubled minds with which he comes in contact.

7. When the Solar Plexus is in active operation and is radiating life, energy and vitality to every part of the body, and to every

"Single entity": now that which was deemed once spiritual or esoteric finds a firm footing in science, namely biology. Here we find the corresponding link between the non-physical and the physical side, opening the 'modus operandi' also to those more inclined to natural sciences.

one whom he meets, the sensations are pleasant, the body is filled with health and all with whom he comes in contact experience a pleasant sensation.

8. If there is any interruption of this radiation the sensations are unpleasant, the flow of life and energy to some part of the body is stopped, and this is the cause of every ill to the human race, physical, mental or emotional.

9. Physical, because the Sun of the body is no longer generating sufficient energy to vitalize some part of the body; mental, because the Conscious Mind is dependent upon the Subconscious Mind for the vitality necessary to support its thoughts, and emotional, because the connection between the Subconscious Mind and the Universal Mind is being interrupted.

10. The Solar Plexus is the point at which the part meets with the whole, **where the Finite becomes infinite**, where the Uncreate becomes create, the Universal becomes individualized, the Invisible becomes visible. It is the point at which life appears and there is no limit to the amount of life an individual may generate from this solar centre.

11. This centre of energy is omnipotent, because it is the point of contact with all life and all intelligence. It can therefore accomplish whatever it is directed to accomplish, and herein lies the power of the Conscious Mind; the Subconscious can and will carry out such plans and ideas as may be suggested to it by the Conscious Mind.

12. Conscious thought, then, is master of this solar centre from which the life and energy of the entire body flows and the quality of the thought which we entertain determines the quality of the thought which this Sun will radiate, and the character of the thought which our Conscious Mind entertains will determine the character of the thought which this Sun will radiate, and the nature of the thought which our Conscious Mind entertains will determine the nature of thought which this Sun will radiate, and consequently will determine the nature of the experience which will result.

13. It is evident, therefore, that all we have to do is **let our light shine**; the more energy we can radiate, the more rapidly

Remember that thought has to be directed consciously, systematically and constructively. It must therefore only express what is true, and that is necessarily harmonious, in order, proportional, beautiful and in its very essence loving.

This is once again a decision you take consciously, and which you will continue to take until it has become part of you.

The man who knows that he has a Solar Plexus will not fear criticism or anything else; he will be too busy radiating courage, confidence, and power; he will anticipate success by his mental attitude.

shall we be enabled to transmute undesirable conditions into sources of pleasure and profit. The important question, then, is how to let this light shine; how to generate this energy?

14. Nonresistant thought expands the Solar Plexus; resistant thought contracts it. Pleasant thought expands it; unpleasant thought contracts it. Thoughts of courage, power, confidence and hope all produce **a corresponding state**, but the one arch enemy of the Solar Plexus which must be absolutely destroyed before there is any possibility of letting any light shine is fear. This enemy must be completely destroyed; he must be eliminated; he must be expelled forever; he is the cloud which hides the Sun; which causes a perpetual gloom.

15. It is this personal devil which makes men fear the past, the present and the future; fear themselves, their friends and their enemies; fear everything and everybody. When fear is effectually and completely destroyed, your light will shine, the clouds will disperse and **you will have found the source of power, energy and life**.

16. When you find that you are really one with the infinite power, and when you can consciously realize this power by a practical demonstration of your ability to overcome any adverse condition by the power of your thought, you will have nothing to fear; fear will have been destroyed and you will have come into possession of your birthright.

17. It is our **attitude of mind** toward life which determines the experiences with which we are to meet; **if we expect nothing, we shall have nothing; if we demand much, we shall receive the greater portion**. The world is harsh only as we fail to assert ourselves. The criticism of the world is bitter only to those who cannot compel room for their ideas.

'Correspondence' is the second of the 7 Hermetic Principles. It is also expressed by saying '"As above, so below." or "As within, so without." In its essence it gives us assurance about the outcome if we know what the cause is.

It also means that your life on Planet Earth is a reflection of what is happening on a planetary and also on a galactic level. The same principles apply. All you have to do is look there and find clues as to what to do in your own life. Astrology and Numerology help you a great deal.

59

It is fear of this criticism that causes many ideas to fail to see the light of day.

18. But the man who knows that he has a Solar Plexus will not fear criticism or anything else; he will be too busy radiating courage, confidence, and power; he will anticipate success by his mental attitude; he will pound barriers to pieces, and leap over the chasm of doubt and hesitation which fear places in his path.

19. A knowledge of our ability to consciously radiate health, strength and harmony will bring us into a realization that there is nothing to fear because we are **in touch with infinite strength**.

20. This knowledge can be gained only **by making practical application of this information**. We learn by doing; through practice the athlete comes powerful.

21. As the following statement is of considerable importance, I will put it in several ways, so that you cannot fail to get the full significance of it. If you are religiously inclined, I would say, you can **let your light shine**. If your mind has a bias toward physical science, I would say **you can wake the Solar Plexus**; or, if you prefer the strictly scientific interpretation, I will say that **you can impress your Subconscious Mind**.

22. I have already told you what the result of this impression will be. It is the method in which you are now interested. You have already learned that the Subconscious is intelligent and that it is creative, and **responsive to the will of the Conscious Mind**. What, then, is the most natural way of making the desired impression? **Mentally concentrate** on the object of your desire; when you are concentrating you are impressing the Subconscious.

23. This is not the only way, but it is a simple and effective way, and the most direct way, and consequently the way in which the best results are secured. It is the method which is producing such extraordinary results that many think that miracles are being accomplished.

24. It is the method by which every great inventor, every great financier, every great statesman has been enabled to convert

This is where most failures occur. Reading this is not enough. It has to be applied, not only through the exercises, but also in real life. You've got to keep doing it over and over again until you have gained mastery.

You have to keep asserting yourself, because it is a vibratory Universe, and resonance can only occur if there is something to resonate with, which would be your thoughts of courage, determination, beauty, compassion, wealth, health, etc.

Be bold! Be courageous! Be daring! There is nothing to lose. All you think you can lose has either not been yours to begin with, or would deteriorate and one day disappear anyway. And if you don't ask, you cannot receive, so make it a habit of asserting your claims. More of that in Part Five!

the subtle and invisible force of desire, faith and confidence into actual, tangible, concrete facts in the objective world.

25. The Subconscious Mind is a part of the Universal Mind. **The Universal is the creative principle of the Universe**, a part must be the same in kind and quality as the whole. This means that this creative power is **absolutely unlimited**; it is not bound by precedent of any kind, and consequently has no prior existing pattern by which to apply its constructive principle.

26. We have found that the Subconscious Mind is responsive to our Conscious Will, which means that the unlimited creative power of the Universal Mind is within control of the Conscious Mind of the individual.

27. When making a practical application of this principle, in accordance with the exercises given in the subsequent lessons, it is well to remember that it is not necessary to outline the method by which the Subconscious will produce the results you desire. The finite can not inform the Infinite. **You are simply to say what you desire, not how you are to obtain it.**

The reason for this is that if you knew how, you would already be on your way. But as you don't yet know, you cannot but simply state your desire and allow the Infinite Intelligence to convert it into tangible vales for and through you.

28. You are the channel by which the undifferentiated is being differentiated, and this differentiation is being accomplished by appropriation. **It only requires recognition** to set causes in motion which will bring about results in accordance with your desire, and this is accomplished because the Universal can act only through the individual, and the individual can act only through the Universal; they are one.

29. For your exercise this week, I will ask you to go one step further. I want you to not only be perfectly still, and inhibit all thought as far as possible, but relax, let go, let the muscles take their normal condition; this will remove all pressure from the nerves, and eliminate that tension which so frequently produces physical exhaustion.

First it was physical control. Then it was mental control. Now it's physical relaxation. There you can already detect the logical sequence of these exercises, leading you to mastery of your own life.

30. Physical relaxation is **a voluntary exercise of the will** and the exercise will be found to be of great value, as it enables the blood to circulate freely to and from the brain and body.

31. Tensions leads to mental unrest and abnormal mental activity of the mind; it produces worry, care, fear and

anxiety. **Relaxation is therefore an absolute necessity in order to allow the mental faculties to exercise the greatest freedom.**

32. Make this exercise as thorough and complete as possible, mentally determine that you will relax every muscle and nerve, until you feel quiet and restful and at peace with yourself and the world.

33. The Solar Plexus will then be ready to function and you will be surprised at the result.

"When any object or purpose is clearly held in thought, its precipitation, in tangible and visible form, is merely a question of time. The vision always precedes and itself determines the realization."
— LILLIAN WHITING

PART THREE — QUESTIONS AND ANSWERS

21. *What system of nerves is the organ of the Conscious Mind?*
The cerebrospinal.

22. *What system of nerves is the organ of the Subconscious Mind?*
The sympathetic.

23. *What is the central point of distribution for energy which the body is constantly generating?*
The Solar Plexus.

24. *How may this distribution be interrupted?*
By resistant, critical, discordant thoughts, but especially fear.

25. *What is the result of such interruption?*
Every ill with which the human race is afflicted.

26. *How may this energy be controlled and directed?*
By conscious thought.

27. *How may fear be completely eliminated?*
By an understanding and recognition of the true source of all power.

28. *What determines the experiences with which we meet in life?*
Our predominant mental attitude.

29. *How may we awake the Solar Plexus?*
Mentally concentrate upon the condition which we desire to see manifested in our lives.

30. *What is the creative principle of the Universe?*
The Universal Mind.

4

THE TRUE »I«

PART FOUR

Enclosed herewith I hand you Part Four. This part will show you why what you think, or do, or feel, is an indication of what you are.

Thought is energy and energy is power, and it is because all the religions, sciences and philosophies with which the world has heretofore been familiar have been based upon the manifestation of this energy instead of the energy itself, that the world has been limited to effects, while causes have been ignored or misunderstood.

For this reason we have God and the Devil in religion, positive and negative in science, and good and bad in philosophy.

The Master Key reverses the process; it is **interested only in the cause**, and the letters received from students tell a marvellous story; they indicate conclusively that students are finding the cause whereby they may secure for themselves health, harmony, abundance, and whatever else may be necessary for their welfare and happiness.

Life is expressive and **it is our business to express ourselves harmoniously and constructively**. Sorrow, misery, unhappiness, disease and poverty are not necessities and we are constantly eliminating them.

But this process of eliminating consists in rising above and beyond limitation of any kind. He who has strengthened and purified his thought need not concern himself about microbes, and he who has come into an understanding of the Law of Abundance will go at once to the source of supply. It is thus that fate, fortune, and destiny will be controlled as readily as a captain controls his ship, or an engineer his train.

When a mind becomes mature, it understands that the germ of defeat is in every selfish thought.

THE TRUE »I«

1. The »I« of you is not the physical body; that is simply an instrument which the »I« uses to carry out its purposes; the »I« cannot be the mind, for the mind is simply another instrument which the »I« uses with which to think, reason, and plan.

2. The »I« must be something which controls and directs both the body and the mind; something which determines what they shall do and how they shall act. When you come into a realization of the true nature of this »I«, you will enjoy **a sense of power** which you have never before known.

3. Your personality is made up of countless individual characteristics, peculiarities, habits, and traits of character; these are the result of your **former** method of thinking, but they have nothing to do with the real »I.«

4. When you say »I think« the »I« tells the mind what it shall think; when you say »I go« the »I« tells the physical body where it shall go; the real nature of this »I« is spiritual, and is the source of the real power which comes to men and women when they come into a realization of their true nature.

5. The greatest and most marvellous power which this »I« has been given is **the power to think**, but few people know how to think constructively, or correctly, consequently they achieve only indifferent results. Most people allow their thoughts to dwell on selfish purposes, the inevitable result of an infantile mind. When a mind becomes mature, it understands that the germ of defeat is in every selfish thought.

6. The trained mind knows that **every transaction must benefit every person who is in any way connected with the transaction**, and any attempt to profit by the weakness, ignorance or necessity of another will inevitably operate to his disadvantage.

7. This is because the individual is a part of the Universal. A part cannot antagonize any other part, but, on the contrary, **the welfare of each part depends upon a recognition of the interest of the whole**.

8. Those who recognize this principle have a great advantage in the affairs of life. They do not wear themselves out. They

Try to come into a thorough understanding of the true nature of the »I«; if you do, you will become invincible!

can eliminate vagrant thoughts with facility. They can readily concentrate to the highest possible degree on any subject. They do not waste time or money upon objects which can be of no possible benefit to them.

9. If you cannot do these things it is because you have thus far not made the necessary effort. Now is the time to make the effort. The result will be exactly in proportion to the effort expended. One of the strongest affirmations which you can use for the purpose of strengthening the will and realizing your power to accomplish, is: »**I can be what I will to be.**«

This means by making use of your will power, read: concentration, you will help bring those things into manifestation that you make the sole centre of your attention, and which you subsequently imbue with feelings, or life-force through the Law of Love.

In practical terms this means showing positive emotions to others, as they will return to you manifold.

10. Every time you repeat it realize who and what this »I« is; try to come into a thorough understanding of the true nature of the »I«; if you do, you will become invincible; that is, provided that your objects and purposes are constructive and are therefore **in harmony with the creative principle of the Universe**.

11. If you make use of this affirmation, **use it continuously**, night and morning, and as often during the day as you think of it, and continue to do so until it becomes a part of you; form the habit.

12. Unless you do this, you had better not start at all, because modern psychology tells us that when we start something and do not complete it, or make a resolution and do not keep it, we are forming the habit of failure; absolute, ignominious failure. If you do not intend to do a thing, do not start; if you do start, see it through even if the heavens fall; if you make up your mind to do something, do it; let nothing, no one, interfere; the »I« in you has determined, the thing is settled; the die is cast, there is no longer any argument.

13. If you carry out this idea, **beginning with small things which you know you can control and **gradually increase**

the effort, but never under any circumstances allowing your »I« to be overruled, you will find that you can eventually **control yourself**, and many men and women have found to their sorrow that it is easier to control a kingdom that to control themselves.

14. But when you have learned to control yourself you will have found the »World Within« which controls the world without; you will have become irresistible; men and things will respond to your every wish without any apparent effort on your part.

15. This is not so strange or impossible as it may appear when you remember that the »World Within« is controlled by the »I« and that this »I« is a part or one with the Infinite »I« which is the Universal Energy or Spirit, usually called God.

16. This is not a mere statement or theory made for the purpose of confirming or establishing an idea, but it is a fact which has been accepted by the best religious thought as well as the best scientific thought.

17. Herbert Spender said: »Amid all the mysteries by which we are surrounded, nothing is more certain than that we are ever in the presence of an Infinite and Eternal Energy from which all things proceed.«

18. Lyman Abbott, in an address delivered before the Alumni of Bangor Theological Seminary, said: »We are coming to think of God as dwelling in man rather than as operating on men from without.«

19. Science goes a little way in its search and stops. Science finds the ever-present Eternal Energy, but Religion finds the Power behind this energy and locates it within man. But this is by no means a new discovery; the Bible says exactly the same thing, and the language is just as plain and convincing: »Know ye not that **ye are the temple of the living God**?« Here, then, is the secret of the wonderful creative power of the »World Within.«

20. Here is the secret of power, of mastery. To overcome does not mean to go without things. Self-denial is not success. We cannot give unless we get; we cannot be helpful unless we are strong. **The Infinite is not a bankrupt** and we who are the

Although there is an Infinite Energy and Infinite Intelligence, it is at the same time based within each of us, and we are calling it forth through our very own thinking – our asking the question; our demand; our prayer or meditation. Yet if we don't think for ourselves and thus fail to make the claim, we will continue to receive only that which others have thought up for us, and that may be unacceptable or to our detriment.

representatives of Infinite power should not be bankrupts either, and if we wish to be of service to others we must have power and more power, but to get it we must give it; **we must be of service**.

21. The more we give the more we shall get; **we must become a channel whereby the Universal can express activity**. The Universal is constantly seeking to express itself, to be of service, and it seeks the channel whereby it can find the greatest activity, where it can do the most good, where it can be of greatest service to mankind.

22. The Universal cannot express through you as long as you are busy with your plans, your own purposes. **Quiet the senses, seek inspiration, focus the mental activity on the within**, dwell in the consciousness of your unity with Omnipotence. »Still water runs deep;« contemplate the multitudinous opportunities to which you have spiritual access by the Omnipresence of power.

23. Visualize the events, circumstances and conditions which these spiritual connections may assist in manifesting. Realize the fact that **the essence and soul of all things is spiritual** and that the spiritual is the real, because it is the life of all there is; when the spirit is gone, the life is gone; it is dead; it has ceased to exist.

24. These mental activities pertain to the world within, to the world of cause; and conditions and circumstances which result are the effect. It is thus that you become a creator. This is **important work**, and the higher, loftier, grander and more noble ideals which you can conceive, the more important the work will become.

25. Over-work or over-play or over-bodily activity of any kind produces conditions of mental apathy and stagnation which makes it impossible to do the more important work which results in a realization of conscious power. We should, therefore, **seek the Silence frequently.** Power comes through repose; it is in the Silence that we can be still, and when we are still, we can think, and thought is the secret of all attainment.

Mental strength is secured in exactly the same way that physical strength is secured: by exercise.

26. Thought is a mode of motion and is carried by the Law of Vibration the same as light or electricity. It is given vitality by the emotions through the Law of Love; it takes form and expression by the Law of Growth; it is a product of the spiritual »I«, hence its Divine, spiritual, and creative nature.

The Law of Love means two things having an attraction for each other with the intention of creating more of their mutual qualities.

27. From this it is evident that in order to express power, abundance or any other constructive purpose, **the emotions must be called upon** to give feeling to the thought so that it will take form. How may this purpose be accomplished? This is the vital point; how may we develop the faith, the courage, the feeling, which will result in accomplishment?

28. The reply is, by exercise; mental strength is secured in exactly the same way that physical strength is secured: by exercise. We think something, perhaps with difficulty the first time; we think the same thing again, and it becomes easier this time; we think it again and again; it then becomes a mental habit. We continue to think the same thing; finally it becomes automatic; we can no longer help thinking this thing; we are now positive of what we think; there is no longer any doubt about it. We are sure; we know.

29. Last week I asked you to relax, to let go physically. This week, I am going to ask you to **let go mentally**. If you practiced the exercise given you last week fifteen or twenty minutes a day in accordance with the instructions, you can no doubt relax physically; and anyone who cannot consciously do this quickly and completely is not a master of himself. He has not obtained freedom; he is still a slave to conditions. But I shall assume that you have mastered the exercise and are ready to take the next step, which is mental freedom.

This is the 4th and final preparation for the next chapters. Mental relaxation allows you to let go of all thoughts. You have to do this in order to stop giving negative thoughts undue attention. After all, energy follows attention, and you cannot expect to receive new things if you keep entertaining the same old thoughts. Remember that the inner world governs the outer world, and the inner world is governed by thought.

30. This week, after taking your usual position, remove all tension by completely relaxing, then mentally let go of all adverse conditions, such as hatred, anger, worry, jealousy, envy, sorrow, trouble or disappointment of any kind.

31. You may say that you cannot »let go« of these things, but you can; you can do so by mentally determining to do so, by voluntary **intention** and **persistence**.

32. The reason that some cannot do this is because they allow themselves to be controlled by the emotions instead of by their intellect. But those who will be guided by the intellect will gain the victory. You will not succeed the first time you try, but **practice makes perfect**, in this as in everything else. You must succeed in dismissing, eliminating and completely destroying these negative and destructive thoughts, because they are the seed which is constantly germinating into discordant conditions of every conceivable kind and description.

"There is nothing truer than that the quality of thought which we entertain correlates certain externals in the outside world. This is the Law from which there is no escape. And it is this Law, this correlative of the thought with its object, that from time immemorial has led the people to believe in special providence."
— WILMANS

31. *What is thought?*
Thought is spiritual energy.

32. *How is it carried?*
By the Law of Vibration.

33. *How is it given vitality?*
By the Law of Love.

34. *How does it take form?*
By the Law of Growth.

35. *What is the secret of its creative power?*
It is a spiritual activity.

36. *How may we develop the faith, courage, and enthusiasm which will result in accomplishment?*
By a recognition of our spiritual nature.

37. *What is the secret of Power?*
Service.

38. *Why is this so?*
Because we get what we give.

39. *What is the Silence?*
A physical stillness.

40. *Of what value is it?*
It is the first step to self-control, self-mastery.

5

CONSCIOUSNESS AS THE CENTRE OF YOUR BEING

PART FIVE

Enclosed herewith you will find Part Five. After studying this part carefully, you will see that every conceivable force or object or fact is the result of mind in action.

Mind in action is thought, and thought is creative. Men are thinking now as they never thought before. Therefore, this is a creative age, and the world is awarding its richest prizes to the thinkers.

Matter is powerless, passive, inert. Mind is force, energy, power. Mind shapes and controls matter. Every form which matter takes is but the expression of some preexisting thought.

But thought works no magic transformations; it obeys natural laws; it sets in motion natural forces; it releases natural energies; it manifests in your conduct and actions, and these in turn react upon your friends and acquaintances, and eventually upon the whole of your environment.

You can originate thought, and, since thoughts are creative, you can create for yourself the things you desire.

CONSCIOUSNESS AS THE CENTRE OF YOUR BEING

1. At least ninety per cent of our mental life is subconscious, so that those who fail to make use of this mental power live within very narrow limits.

2. The Subconscious can and will solve any problem for us if we know how to direct it. The subconscious processes are always at work; the only question is: are we to be simply passive recipients of this activity, or are we to consciously direct the work? Shall we have a vision of the destination to be reached, the dangers to be avoided, or shall we simply drift?

IMPORTANT: This implies that the Infinite Intelligence is already part of your Being. You cannot but find it on the inside!

3. We have found that **Mind pervades every part of the physical body** and is always capable of being directed or impressed by authority coming from the objective or the more dominant portion of the mind.

4. The mind, which pervades the body, is largely the result of heredity, which, in turn, is simply the result of all the environments of all past generations on the responsive and ever-

The Law of Attraction brings us »our own«, the things which we have created by our thought processes, whether consciously or unconsciously.

moving life forces. An understanding of this fact will **enable us to use our authority** when we find some undesirable trait of character manifesting.

5. We can consciously use all the desirable characteristics with which we have been provided and **we can repress and refuse to allow the undesirable ones to manifest.**

6. Again, this mind which pervades our physical body is not only the result of hereditary tendencies, but is the result of home, business and social environment, where countless thousands of impressions, ideas, prejudices and similar thoughts have been received. Much of this has been received from others, the result of opinions, suggestions or statements; much of it is the result of our own thinking, but nearly all of it has been **accepted with little or no examination or consideration**.

7. The idea seemed plausible, the Conscious received it, passed it on to the Subconscious, where it was taken up by the Sympathetic System and passed on to be built into our physical body. »The word has become flesh.«

8. This, then, is the way we are consistently creating and recreating ourselves; we are today the result of our past thinking, and **we shall be what we are thinking today**. The Law of Attraction is bringing to us not the things we should like, or the things we wish for, or the things some one else has, but it brings us »our own«, the things which we have created by our thought processes, whether consciously or unconsciously. Unfortunately, many of us are creating these things unconsciously.

9. If either of us were building a home for ourselves, how careful we would be in regard to the plans; how we should study every detail; how we should watch the material and **select only the best of everything**; and yet how careless we are when

Remember that we are talking about your current vibratory makeup, thus in the last instance, matter. As matter is undergoing constant change, a new mental attitude inevitably results in new neural pathways to be formed, therefore a new nervous sensitivity and consequently new effects in your world outside. In other words: no matter what or who you have become because of outside influences, you can change all that right here, right now. This is a tremendous opportunity!

it comes to building our Mental Home, which is infinitely more important than any physical home, as everything which can possibly enter into our lives depends upon the character of the material which enters into the construction of our Mental Home.

10. What is the character of this material? We have seen that it is the result of the impressions which we have accumulated in the past and stored away in our subconscious Mentality. If these impressions have been of fear, of worry, of care, of anxiety; if they have been despondent, negative, doubtful, then the texture of the material which we are weaving today will be of the same negative material. Instead of being of any value, it will be mildewed and rotten and will bring us only more toil and care and anxiety. We shall be forever busy trying to patch it up and make it appear at least genteel.

11. But if we have stored away nothing but **courageous thought**, if we have been **optimistic**, **positive**, and have immediately thrown any kind of negative thought on the scrap pile, have refused to have anything to do with it, have refused to associate with it or become identified with it in any way, what then is the result? Our mental material is now of the best kind; we can weave any kind of material we want; we can use any colour we wish; we know that the texture is firm, that the material is solid, that it will not fade, and we have no fear, no anxiety concerning the future; there is nothing to cover, there are no patches to hide.

12. These are **psychological facts**; there is no theory or guess work about these thinking processes; there is nothing secret about them; in fact, they are so plain that every one can understand them. The thing to do is to **have a mental house-cleaning**, and to have this house-cleaning every day, and keep the house clean. Mental, moral and physical cleanliness are absolutely indispensable if we are to make progress of any kind.

13. When this mental house-cleaning process has been completed, the material which is left will be suitable for the making of the kind of ideals or mental images which we desire to realize.

78

Mental, moral and physical cleanliness are absolutely indispensable if we are to make progress of any kind.

14. There is a fine estate awaiting a claimant. Its broad acres, with abundant crops, running water and fine timber, stretch away as far as the eye can see. There is a mansion, spacious and cheerful, with rare pictures, a well-stocked library, rich hangings, and every comfort and luxury. All the heir has to do is to assert his heirship, take possession, and use the property. He must use it; he must not let it decay; for **use is the condition** on which he holds it. To neglect it is to lose possession.

Here Charles Haanel refers to the beauty and harmony, the joy and wealth which is the Universal Mind, which you are an integral part of. Everything is there already, but unless you lay claim to it and actually use it, you will not be able to derive any benefit from it. Use is the condition!

15. In the domain of mind and spirit, in the domain of practical power, such an estate is yours. You are the heir! You can assert your heirship and possess, and use this rich inheritance. Power over circumstances is one of its fruits, health, harmony and prosperity are assets upon its balance sheet. It offers you poise and peace. It costs you only the labour of studying and harvesting its great resources. **It demands no sacrifice, except the loss of your limitations, your servitudes, your weakness.** It clothes you with self-honour, and puts a sceptre in your hands.

16. To gain this estate, **three processes are necessary:** You must **earnestly desire** it. You must **assert your claim**. You must **take possession**.

1. Earnestly desire – Ask!
2. Assert your claim – Answer!
3. Take possession – Receive!

17. You admit that those are not burdensome conditions.

18. You are familiar with the subject of heredity. Darwin, Huxley, Haeckel, and other physical scientists have piled evidence mountain high that heredity is a law attending progressive creation. It is progressive heredity which gives man his erect attitude, his power of motion, the organs of digestions, blood circulation, nerve force, muscular force, bone structure and a host of other faculties on the physical side. There are even more impressive facts concerning heredity of mind force. All these constitute what may be called your human heredity.

19. But there is a heredity which the physical scientists have not compassed. It lies beneath and antecedent to all their

All possession is the result of the accumulative attitude of mind, or the money consciousness; this is the magic wand.

researches. At a point where they throw up their hands in despair, saying they cannot account for what they see, this divine heredity is found in full sway.

20. It is the benignant force which decrees primal creation. It thrills down from the Divine, direct into every created being. It originates life, which the physical scientist has not done, nor ever can do. It stands out among all forces supreme, unapproachable. No human heredity can approach it. No human heredity measures up to it.

21. **This Infinite Life flows through you; is you.** Its doorways are but the faculties which comprise your consciousness. To keep open these doors is the Secret of Power. Is it not worth while to make the effort?

22. The great fact is, that the source of all life and all power is from within. Persons, circumstances and events may suggest need and opportunities, but the insight, strength and power to answer these needs will be found within.

23. Avoid counterfeits. **Build firm foundations for your consciousness** upon forces which flow direct from the Infinite source, the Universal Mind of which you are the image and likeness.

24. Those we have come into possession of this inheritance are never quite the same again. They have come into possession of **a sense of power** hitherto undreamed of. They can never again be timid, weak, vacillating, or fearful. They are indissolubly connected with Omnipotence. Something in them has been aroused; they have suddenly discovered that they possess a **tremendous latent ability** of which they were heretofore entirely unconscious.

25. **This power is from within, but we cannot receive it unless we give it.** Use is the condition upon which we hold this inheritance. We are each of us but the channel through which the Omnipotent power is being differentiated into

Giving is a mental process. You can simply decree to give someone wealth, health and happiness. This, as you will learn in Part 24, will put you in spiritual connection with that person. And through the use mentioned earlier in this Part, you will develop your consciousness and therefore increase the benefits you derive from it. This is why you cannot afford but to think harmonious thoughts.

form; unless we give, the channel is obstructed and we can receive no more. This is true on every plane of existence and in every field of endeavour and all walks of life. The more we give, the more we get. The athlete who wishes to get strong must make use of the strength he has, and the more he gives the more he will get. The financier who wishes to make money must make use of the money he has, for only by using it can he get more.

26. The merchant who does not keep his goods going out will soon have none coming in; the corporation which fails to give efficient service will soon lack customers; the attorney who fails to get results will soon lack clients, and so it goes everywhere; **power is contingent upon a proper use of the power already in our possession**; what is true in every field of endeavour, every experience in life, is true of the power from which every other power known among men is begotten — spiritual power. Take away the spirit and what is left? Nothing.

27. If then the spirit is all there is, upon the recognition of this fact must depend the ability to demonstrate all power, whether physical, mental or spiritual.

28. All possession is the result of the **accumulative attitude of mind**, or the money consciousness; this is the magic wand which will enable you to **receive the idea**, and it will **formulate plans for you to execute**, and you will find as much pleasure in the execution as in the satisfaction of attainment and achievement.

29. Now, go to your room, take the same seat, the same position as heretofore, and mentally select a place which has pleasant associations. Make a complete mental picture of it, see the buildings, the grounds, the trees, friends, associations, everything complete. At first, you will find yourself thinking of everything under the Sun, except the ideal upon which you desire to concentrate. But do not let that discourage you. **Persistence will win**, but persistence requires that **you practice these exercises every day without fail**.

This is the first of a series of visualization exercises. The first four parts prepared the ground, and now that you can control and relax yourself both physically and mentally, you are ready to create new images in your mind. The following parts will gradually increase your visualization skills, from the simple to the completely abstract and highly symbolic.

He who walks the PATH OF LIGHT is marked by:

*1. COMPASSION: for he understands the
Needs of the Weary Animal, the Sorrows of
the Child, and the Mind of the Stranger.*

*2. HARMONY OF SOUL: for his Eye perceives
Nature, his Heart comprehends Nature, and his
Courage enables him to dwell with Nature.*

*3. SKILL IN ACTION: for he Loves
his Work, he Knows his Work, and he
Works with Will for no reward.*

*4. UNIVERSAL VISION: for he loves
all things, he is just to all beings, and
he serves the Law with gladness.*

*O my son, when the Marks of True Manhood
are engraved in the Substance of your
Being, you will ask no more for Knowledge, nor will you crave to possess it, because
you will be KNOWLEDGE ITSELF.*

*Ngisis kuve hambaseke kahlese!
(Follow thou after Peace).*

— FROM "THE SAYINGS OF THE ANCIENT
ONE" BY P. G. BOWEN, ONE OF THE GREATEST
WRITINGS TO COME OUT OF AFRICA

41. *What proportion of our mental life is subconscious?*
At least ninety percent.

42. *Is this vast mental storehouse generally utilized?*
No.

43. *Why not?*
Few understand or appreciate the fact that it is an activity which they may consciously direct.

44. *Where has the Conscious Mind received its governing tendencies?*
From heredity — which means that it is the result of all the environments of all past generations.

45. *What is the Law of Attraction bringing to us?*
Our »Own.«

46. *What is our »Own«?*
What we inherently are, and is the result of our past thinking, both conscious and subconscious.

47. *Of what is the material with which we construct our mental home composed?*
The thoughts which we entertain.

48. *What is the Secret of Power?*
A recognition of the omnipresence of omnipotence.

49. *Where does it originate?*
All life and all power is from within.

50. *Upon what is the possession of power contingent?*
Upon a proper use of the power already in our possession.

6

FROM AWARENESS TO SUCCESS

It is my privilege to enclose Part Six. This part will give you an excellent understanding of the most wonderful piece of mechanism which has ever been created. A mechanism whereby you may create for yourself Health, Strength, Success, Prosperity or any other condition which you desire. Necessities are demands, and **demands create action**, and actions bring about results. The process of evolution is constantly building our tomorrows out of our todays. Individual development, like universal development, must be **gradual** with an ever increasing capacity and volume.

The knowledge that if we infringe upon the rights of others, we become moral thorns and find ourselves entangled at every turn of the road, should be an indication that **success is contingent upon the highest moral ideal**, which is »The greatest good to the greatest number.«

Aspiration, desire and harmonious relations constantly and persistently maintained will accomplish results. The greatest hindrance is erroneous and fixed ideas.

To be in tune with eternal truth we must possess poise and harmony within. In order to receive intelligence the receiver must be in tune with the transmitter.

Thought is a product of mind and mind is creative, but this does not mean that the Universal will change its modus operandi to suit us or our ideas, but it does mean that **we can come into harmonious relationship with the Universal**, and when we have accomplished this we may ask anything to which we are entitled, and the way will be made plain.

FROM AWARENESS TO SUCCESS

1. The Universal Mind is so wonderful that it is difficult to understand its utilitarian powers and possibilities and its unlimited producing effects.

2. We have found that this mind is not only all intelligence but all substance. How, then, is it to be differentiated in form? How are we to secure the effect which we desire?

Without action no demand can be fulfilled. It will remain a thought far too weak to attract anything from the spiritual realm.

Keep this in mind at all times: "The highest moral ideal."

86

3.   Ask any electrician what the effect of electricity will be and he will reply that »Electricity is a form of motion and its effect will depend upon the mechanism to which it is attached.« Upon this mechanism will depend whether we shall have heat, light, power, music or any of the other marvellous demonstration of power to which this vital energy has been harnessed.

4.   What effect can be produced by thought? The reply is that **thought is mind in motion** (just as wind is air in motion), and its effect will depend entirely on the »mechanism to which it is attached.«

5.   Here, then, is the secret of all mental power: it depends entirely on the mechanism which we attach.

6.   What is this mechanism? You know something of the mechanism which has been invented by Edison, Bell, Marconi and other electrical wizards, by which place and space and time have become only figures of speech, but did you ever stop to think that the mechanism which has been given you for transforming the Universal, Omnipresent Potential Power was invented by a greater inventor than Edison?

7.   We are accustomed to examining the mechanism of the implements which we use for tilling the soil, and we try to get an understanding of the mechanism of the automobile which we drive, but most of us are content to remain in absolute ignorance of **the greatest piece of mechanism which as ever come into existence, the brain of man**.

8.   Let us examine the wonders of this mechanism; perhaps we shall thereby get a better understanding of the various effects of which it is the cause.

9.   In the first place, there is the great mental world in which we live and move and have our being; this world is omnipotent, omniscient and omnipresent; it will respond to our desire **in direct ratio** to our purpose and faith; the purpose must be in accordance with the law of our being, that is, it must be creative or constructive. Our faith must be strong enough to generate a current of sufficient strength to bring our purpose into manifestation. »As thy faith is, so be it unto thee,« bears the stamp of scientific test.

This is the meaning of 'you cannot express powers that you do not possess'. For example, the human hearing range is between 20 and 38.000 hz. Above and below that there is silence, but dogs for instance can hear those higher frequencies too. So it is our readying the field for thoughts (vibrations) of beauty, love, health and wealth that will make those things come to us. It physically cannot work any other way.

10. The effects which are produced in the world without are the result of the action and reaction of the Individual upon the Universal; that is the process which we call thinking; the brain is the organ through which this process is accomplished; think of the wonder of it all! Do you love music, flowers, literature, or are you inspired by the thought of ancient or modern genius? Remember, every beauty to which you respond must have its **corresponding outline in your brain** before you can appreciate it.

11. There is not a single virtue or principle in the storehouse of nature which the brain cannot express. **The brain is an embryonic world**, ready to develop at any time as necessity may arise. If you can comprehend that this is a scientific truth and one of the wonderful laws of nature, it will be easier for you to get an understanding of the mechanism by which these extraordinary results are being accomplished.

12. The nervous system has been compared to an electric circuit with its battery of cells in which force is originated, and its white matter to insulated wires by which the current is conveyed; it is through these channels that every impulse or desire is carried through the mechanism.

13. The spinal cord is the great motor and sensory pathway by which messages are conveyed to and from the brain; then, there is the blood supply plunging through the veins and arteries, renewing our energy and strength, the perfectly arranged structure upon which the entire physical body rests, and, finally, the delicate and beautiful skin, clothing the entire mechanism is a mantle of beauty.

14. This then is the »Temple of the living God« and the individual »I« is given control and upon his **understanding**

A perfect conception and understanding of the laws governing in the mental world cannot fail to be of inestimable value in the transaction of business.

of the mechanism which is within his control will the result depend.

15. Every thought sets the brain cells in action; at first the substance upon which the thought is directed fails to respond, but if the thought is sufficiently refined and concentrated, the substance finally yields and expresses perfectly.

16. This influence of the mind can be exerted upon any part of the body, causing the elimination of any undesirable effect.

17. A perfect conception and understanding of the laws governing in the mental world cannot fail to be of inestimable value in the transaction of business, as it develops the power of discernment and gives a clearer understanding and appreciation of facts.

18. The man who looks within instead of without cannot fail to make use of the mighty forces which will eventually determine his course in life and so bring him into vibration with all that is best, strongest and most desirable.

19. **Attention or concentration is probably the most important essential in the development of mind culture.** The possibilities of attention when properly directed are so startling that they would hardly appear credible to the uninitiated. The cultivation of attention is the distinguishing characteristic of every successful man or woman, and is the very highest personal accomplishment which can be acquired.

20. The power of attention can be more readily understood by comparing it with a magnifying glass in which the rays of sunlight are focused. They possess no particular strength as long as the glass is moved about and the rays directed from one place to another, but let the glass be held perfectly still and let the rays be focused on one spot for any length of time, the effect will become immediately apparent.

21. So with the power of thought. Let power be dissipated by scattering the thought from one object to another, and no result is apparent, but focus this power through **attention or concentration** on any single purpose for any length of time and nothing becomes impossible.

22. A very simple remedy for a very complex situation, some will say. All right, try it, you who have had no experience in

concentrating the thought on a definite purpose or object. Choose any single object and concentrate your attention on it for a definite purpose for even ten minutes; you cannot do it; the mind will wander a dozen times and it will be necessary to bring it back to the original purpose, and each time the effect will have been lost and at the end of the ten minutes nothing will have been gained, because you have not been able to hold your thought steadily to the purpose.

23. It is, however, through attention that you will finally be able to overcome of obstacles of any kind that appear in your path onward and upward, and the only way to acquire this wonderful power is by practice — **practice makes perfect**, in this as in anything else.

24. In order to cultivate the power of attention, bring a photograph with you to the same seat in the same room in the same position as heretofore. Examine it closely at least ten minutes, note the expression of the eyes, the form of the features, the clothing, the way the hair is arranged; in fact, note every detail shown on the photograph carefully. Now cover it and close your eyes and try to see it mentally; if you can see every detail perfectly and can form a good mental image of the photograph, you are to be congratulated. If not, repeat the process until you can.

25. This step is simply for the purpose of preparing the soil; next week we shall be ready to sow the seed.

26. It is by such exercises as these that you will finally be able to **control your mental moods, your attitude, your consciousness**.

27. Great financiers are learning to withdraw from the multitude more and more, that they may have more time for planning, thinking and generating the right mental moods.

Attention or concentration is probably the most important essential in the development of your mind.

90

A single idea may be worth millions of dollars, and these ideas can only come to those who are receptive, who are prepared to receive them, who are in a successful frame of mind.

28. Successful businessmen are constantly demonstrating the fact that **it pays to keep in touch with the thought of other successful business men**.

29. A single idea may be worth millions of dollars, and these ideas can only come to those who are receptive, who are prepared to receive them, who are in a successful frame of mind.

30. Men are learning to place themselves in harmony with the Universal Mind; they are learning the unity of all things; they are learning the basic methods and principles of thinking, and this is changing conditions and multiplying results.

31. They are finding that circumstances and environment follow the trend of mental and spiritual progress; they find that growth follows knowledge; action follows inspiration; opportunity follows perception; **always the spiritual first**, then the transformation into the infinite and illimitable possibilities of achievement.

32. As the individual is but the **channel** for the differentiation of the Universal, these possibilities are necessarily inexhaustible.

33. Thought is the process by which we may absorb the Spirit of Power, and hold the result in our inner consciousness until it becomes a part of our ordinary consciousness. The method of accomplishing this result by the **persistent practice of a few fundamental principles**, as explained in this System, is the Master Key which unlocks the storehouse of Universal Truth.

34. The two great sources of human suffering at present are bodily disease and mental anxiety. These may be readily traced to **the infringement of some Natural Law**. This is, no doubt, owing to the fact that so far knowledge has largely

You have to apply the same principle to your own life. If you want to become successful, you will have to go to where successful people meet – irrespective of the kind of success you are striving for. It's an energetic thing first and foremost, and remember that ideas are simply energy, so if you want to go into resonance with success, seek out the places and people that represent success for you.

This will help those with a Christian religious background, who usually struggle with the idea that the person is the source of all power. Charles Haanel makes it clear that although we are just the channel of expression, it is still our thinking that is the deciding factor. There is only one consciousness that can think!

91

remained partial, but the clouds of darkness which have accumulated through long ages are beginning to roll away and with them many of the miseries that attend imperfect information.

"That a man can change himself, improve himself, re-create himself, control his environment, and master his own destiny is the conclusion of every mind who is wide-awake to the power of rightful thought in constructive action."
— LARSON

51. *What are some of the effects which can
    be produced by electricity?*
    Heat, light, power, music.

52. *Upon what do these various effects depend?*
    Upon the mechanism to which electricity is attached.

53. *What is the result of the action and interaction
    of the Individual Mind upon the Universal?*
    The conditions and experiences with which we meet.

54. *How may these conditions be changed?*
    By changing the mechanism by which the
    Universal is differentiated in form.

55. *What is this mechanism?*
    The brain.

56. *How may it be changed?*
    By the process we call thinking. Thoughts
    produce brain cells, and these cells respond to
    the corresponding thought in the Universal.

57. *Of what value is the power of concentration?*
    It is the very highest personal accomplishment
    which can be acquired, and the distinguishing
    characteristic of every successful man or woman.

58. *How may it be acquired?*
    By faithfully practicing the exercises in this System.

59. *Why is this so important?*
    Because it will enable us to control our thoughts, and
    since thoughts are causes conditions must be effects; if
    we can control the cause we can also control the effect.

60. *What is changing conditions and multiplying
    results in the objective world?*
    Men are learning the basic methods
    of constructive thinking.

7

THE POWER OF YOUR IMAGINATION

PART SEVEN

Through all the ages man has believed in an invisible power, through which and by which all things have been created and are continually being re-created.

We may personalize this power and call it God, or we may think of it as the essence or spirit, which permeates all things, but in either case **the effect is the same**.

So far as the individual is concerned, the objective, the physical, the visible, is the personal, that which can be cognized by the senses. It consists of body, brain and nerves. The subjective is the spiritual, the invisible, the impersonal.

The personal is conscious because it is a personal entity. **The impersonal**, being the same in kind and quality as all other Being, **is not conscious of itself** and has therefore been termed the Subconscious. The personal, or Conscious, has the power of will and choice, and can therefore exercise discrimination in the selection of methods whereby to bring about the solution of difficulties. The impersonal, or spiritual, being a part or one with the source, and origin of all power, can necessarily exercise no such choice, but, on the contrary, it has infinite resources at its command. It can and does bring about results by methods concerning which the human or Individual Mind can have no possible conception.

You will therefore see that it is your privilege to depend upon the human will with all its limitations and misconceptions, or you may **utilize the potentialities of Infinity by making use of the Subconscious Mind**. Here, then, is the scientific explanation of the wonderful power which has been put within your control, if you but understand, appreciate and recognize it.

One method of consciously utilizing this omnipotent power is outlined in Part Seven.

THE POWER OF YOUR IMAGINATION

I. Visualization is the process of making **mental images**, and the image is the mould or model which will serve as a pattern from which your future will emerge.

This utilization is effected through intuition. Again, the purpose of this course is to awaken and strengthen your intuitive faculties, because other than your Conscious Mind, you can rely on your Subconscious Mind. This cannot be stressed often enough, as it is only through silent thought concentration that we awaken our intuitive powers.

96

2. Make the pattern clear and make it beautiful; do not be afraid; make it grand; remember that no limitation can be placed upon you by any one but yourself; you are not limited as to cost or material; draw on the Infinite for your supply, **construct it in your imagination**; it will have to be there before it will ever appear anywhere else.

3. Make the image clear and clean-cut, hold it firmly in the mind and you will gradually and constantly bring the thing nearer to you. You can be what »you will to be.«

4. This is another psychological fact which is well known, but unfortunately, reading about it will not bring about any result which you may have in mind; it will not even help you to form the mental image, much less bring it into manifestation. **Work is necessary – labour, hard mental labour, the kind of effort which so few are willing to put forth**.

5. The first step is **idealization**. It is likewise the most important step, because it is the plan on which you are going to build. It must be solid; it must be permanent. The architect, when he plans a 30-story building, has every line and detail pictured in advance. The engineer, when he spans a chasm, first ascertains the strength requirements of a million separate parts.

6. They see the end before a single step is taken; so you are to picture in your Mind what you want; you are sowing the seed, but before sowing any seed you want to know what the harvest is to be. This is idealization. If you are not sure, return to the chair daily until the picture becomes plain; it will gradually unfold; first the general plan will be dim, but it will take shape, the outline will take form, then the **details**, and you will **gradually** develop the power by which you will be enabled to formulate plans which will eventually materialize in the objective world. You will come to know what the future holds for you.

7. Then comes the process of **visualization**. You must see the picture more and more complete, see the detail, and, as the details begin to unfold **the ways and means for bringing it into manifestation will develop**. One thing will lead to another. Thought will lead to action, action will develop

methods, methods will develop friends, and friends will bring about circumstances, and, finally, the third step, or **materialization**, will have been accomplished.

8. We all recognize the Universe must have been thought into shape before it ever could have become a material fact. And if we are willing to follow along the lines of the **Great Architect of the Universe,** we shall find our thoughts taking form, just as the Universe took concrete form. It is the same mind operating through the individual. There is no difference in kind or quality, the only difference is one of degree.

9. The architect visualizes his building, he sees it as he wishes it to be. His thought becomes a plastic mould from which the building will eventually emerge, a high one or a low one, a beautiful one or a plain one, his vision takes form on paper and eventually the necessary material is utilized and the building stands complete.

Nikola Tesla (1856 – 1943)

10. The inventor visualizes his idea in exactly the same manner, for instance, **Nikola Tesla**, he with the giant intellect, one of the greatest inventors of all ages, the man who has brought forth the most amazing realities, always visualizes his inventions before attempting to work them out. He did not rush to embody them in form and then spend his time in correcting defects. Having first built up the idea in his imagination, he held it there as a mental picture, to be reconstructed and improved by his thought. »In this way,« he writes in the *Electrical Experimenter*. »I am enabled to rapidly develop and perfect a conception without touching anything. When I have gone so far as to embody in the invention every possible improvement I can think of, and see no fault anywhere, I put into concrete, the product of my brain. Invariably my devise works as I conceived it should; in twenty years there has not been a single exception.«

11. If you can conscientiously follow these directions, **you will develop Faith**, the kind of Faith that is the »Substance of things hoped for, the evidence of things not seen«; **you will develop confidence**, the kind of confidence that leads to endurance and courage; **you will develop the power of**

concentration which will enable you to exclude all thoughts except the ones which are associated with your purpose.

12. The law is that thought will manifest in form, and only one who knows how to be the **divine thinker of his own thoughts** can ever take a Master's place and **speak with authority**.

13. **Clearness and accuracy are obtained only by repeatedly having the image in mind**. Each repeated action renders the image more clear and accurate than the preceding, and in proportion to the clearness and accuracy of the image will the outward manifestation be. You must build it firmly and securely in your mental world, the world within, before it can take form in the world without. You can build nothing of value, even in the mental world, unless you have the proper material. When you have the material, you can build anything you wish, but make sure of your material. You cannot make broadcloth from shoddy.

14. This material will be brought out by millions of silent mental workers and fashioned into the form of the image which you have in mind.

15. Think of it! You have over *five million* of these mental workers, ready and in active use; brain cells they are called. Besides this, there is another reserve force of at least an equal number, ready to be called into action at the slightest need. Your power to think, then, is almost unlimited, and this means that your power to create the kind of material which is necessary to build for yourself any kind of environment which you desire is practically unlimited.

16. In addition to these millions of mental workers, you have billions of mental workers in the body, every one of which is endowed with **sufficient intelligence to understand and act upon any message or suggestion given**. These cells are all busy creating and recreating the body, but, in addition to this, they are endowed with psychic activity whereby they can attract to themselves the substance necessary for perfect development.

17. They do this by the same law and in the same manner that every form of life attracts to itself the necessary material

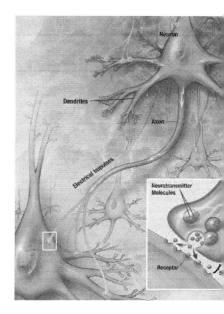

Scheme of a chemical synapse

Wikipedia: The human brain has been estimated to contain 50–100 billion (10^{11}) neurons, of which about 10 billion (10^{10}) are cortical pyramidal cells. These cells pass signals to each other via as many as 1000 trillion (10^{15}, 1 quadrillion) synaptic connections.

99

for growth. The oak, the rose, the lily, all require certain material for their most perfect expression and they secure it by **silent demand**, the Law of Attraction, the most certain way for you to secure what you require for your most complete development.

18. Make the mental image; make it clear, distinct, perfect; hold it firmly; **the ways and means will develop**; supply will follow the demand; you will be led to do the right thing at the right time and in the right way. **Earnest Desire** will bring about **Confident Expectation**, and this in turn must be reinforced by **Firm Demand**. These three cannot fail to bring about attainment, because the Earnest Desire is the **feeling**, the Confident Expectation is the **thought**, and the Firm Demand is the **will**, and, as we have seen, feeling gives vitality to thought and the will holds it steadily until the law of Growth brings it into manifestation.

19. Is it not wonderful that man has such tremendous power within himself, such transcendental faculties concerning which he had no conception? Is it not strange that we have always been taught to look for strength and power »without?« We have been taught to look everywhere but »within«, and whenever this power manifested in our lives, we were told that it was something supernatural.

20. There are many who have come to an understanding of this wonderful power, and who make serious and conscientious efforts to realize health, power and other conditions, and seem to fail. They do not seem able to bring the Law into operation. **The difficulty in nearly every case is that they are dealing with externals**. They want money, power, health and abundance, but they fail to realize that these are **effects** and can come only when the cause is found.

Create ideals only; give no thought to external conditions; make the world within beautiful and opulent.

21. Those who will give no attention to the world without **will seek only to ascertain the truth**, will look only for wisdom, will find that this wisdom will unfold and disclose the source of all power, that it will manifest in thought and purpose which will create the external conditions desired. This truth will find expression in noble purpose and courageous action.

22. **Create ideals only**; give no thought to external conditions; **make the world within beautiful and opulent** and the world without will express and manifest the condition which you have within. You will come into a realization of your power to create ideals and these ideals will be projected into the world of effect.

23. For instance, a man is in debt. He will be continually thinking about the debt, concentrating on it, and as thoughts are causes the result is that he not only fastens the debt closer to him, but actually creates more debt. He is putting the great Law of Attraction into operation with the usual and inevitable result — Loss leads to greater »Loss.«

24. What, then, is the correct principle? **Concentrate on the things you want**, not on the things you do not want. **Think of abundance**; idealize the methods and plans for putting the Law of Abundance into operation. Visualize the condition which the Law of Abundance creates; this will result in manifestation.

25. If the law operates perfectly to bring about poverty, lack and every form of limitation for those who are continually entertaining thoughts of lack and fear, it will operate with the same **certainty** to bring about conditions of abundance and opulence for those who entertain thoughts of courage and power.

26. This is a difficult problem for many; we are too anxious; we manifest anxiety, fear, distress; we want to do something; we want to help; we are like a child who has just planted a seed and every fifteen minutes goes and stirs up the Earth to see if it is growing. Of course, under such circumstances, the seed will never germinate, and yet this is exactly what many of us do in the mental world.

In the beginning you lack the necessary brain cells for an abundant life, but concentration will result in the universal substance to yield and in new neural pathways to be built. You are constantly reinventing yourself through your own thinking. Wou will find ample scientific proof to support this claim. Look up "Candace Pert" on Google or Youtube.

The advice to give no thought to external conditions is because these are all effects, and you are to create new causes, new mental images, which in turn result in new effects, new external conditions.

This is where trust, belief and faith come in. Remember that we can be sure of the effect once we have ascertained the cause. This makes things so much easier for us, as the Law works with invariable precision. A sunflower seed will always turn into a sunflower, not an apple tree.

First it was a past event, of which you remembered some details. Then it was a photograph, where you memorized and then recalled the details. Both were passive. This is an active visualization, where something happens in your Mind as a result of your creative imagination.

27. **We must plant the seed and leave it undisturbed**. This does not mean that we are to sit down and do nothing, by no means; we will do more and better work than we have ever done before. New channels will constantly be provided, new doors will open; all that is necessary is to have an open mind, **be ready to act when the time comes**.

28. **Thought force is the most powerful means of obtaining knowledge**, and if concentrated on any subject will solve the problem. Nothing is beyond the power of human comprehension, but in order to harness thought force and make it do your bidding, work is required.

29. Remember that thought is the fire that creates the steam that turns the wheel of fortune, upon which your experiences depend.

30. Ask yourself a few questions and then reverently await the response: Do you not now and then feel the Self within you? Do you assert this Self or do you follow the majority? Remember that **majorities are always led**, they never lead. It was the majority that fought, tooth and nail, against the steam engine, the power loom and every other advance or improvement ever suggested.

31. For your exercise this week, visualize your friend, see him exactly as you last saw him, see the room, the furniture, recall the conversation, now see his face, see it distinctly, now talk to him about some subject of mutual interest; see his expression change, watch him smile. Can you do this? All right, you can. Then arouse his interest; tell him a story of adventure; see his eyes light up with the spirit of fun or excitement. Can you do all of this? If so, your imagination is good, you are making excellent progress.

PART SEVEN — QUESTIONS AND ANSWERS

61. *What is visualization?*
     The process of making mental pictures.

62. *What is the result of this method of thought?*
     By holding the image or picture in mind,
     we can gradually but surely bring the thing
     nearer to us. We can be what we will to be.

63. *What is Idealization?*
     It is a process of visualizing or idealizing the plans which
     will eventually materialize in our objective world.

64. *Why are clearness and accuracy necessary?*
     Because »seeing« creates »feeling« and »feeling«
     creates »being.« First the mental, then the emotional,
     then the illimitable possibilities of achievement.

65. *How are they obtained?*
     Each repeated action renders the image
     more accurate than the former one.

66. *How is the material for the construction
     of your mental image secured?*
     By millions of mental workers. Brain cells they are called.

67. *How are the necessary conditions for bringing about the
     materialization of your ideal in the objective world secured?*
     By the Law of Attraction. The natural law by which
     all conditions and experiences are brought about.

68. *What three steps are necessary in order
     to bring this law into operation?*
     Earnest Desire, Confident Expectation, Firm Demand.

69. *Why do many fail?*
     Because they concentrate on loss, disease and
     disaster. The law is operating perfectly; the
     things they fear are coming upon them.

70. *What is the alternative?*
     Concentrate on the ideals which you desire
     to see manifested in your life.

THE VALUE OF TRUTHFUL THINKING

PART EIGHT

Thomas Carlyle (1795 – 1881)

Ralph Waldo Emerson
(1803 – 1882)

In this Part you will find that you may freely choose what you think but **the result of your thought is governed by an immutable law**! Is not this a wonderful thought? Is it not wonderful to know that our lives are not subject to caprice or variability of any kind? That they are governed by law. **This stability is our opportunity**, because by complying with the law we can secure the desired effect with invariable precision. It is the law which makes the Universe one grand paean of Harmony. If it were not for law, the Universe would be a Chaos instead of a Cosmos.

Here, then, is the secret of the origin of both good and evil, this is all the good and evil there ever was or ever will be.

Let me illustrate. **Thought results in action, if your thought is constructive and harmonious, the result will be good; if your thought is destructive or inharmonious, the result will be evil.**

There is therefore but one law, one principle, one cause, one Source of Power, and good and evil are simply words which have been coined to indicate the result of our action, or our compliance or noncompliance with this law.

The importance of this is well-illustrated in the lives of **Ralph Waldo Emerson** and **Thomas Carlyle**. Emerson loved the good and his life was a symphony of peace and harmony, Carlyle hated the bad, and his life was a record of perpetual discord and inharmony.

Here we have two grand men, each intent upon achieving the same ideal, but one makes use of constructive thought and is therefore in harmony with Natural Law, the other makes use of destructive thought and therefore brings upon himself discord of every kind and character.

It is evident therefore that **we are to hate nothing**, not even the »bad«, because hatred is destructive, and we shall soon find that by entertaining destructive thought we are sowing the »wind« and in turn shall reap the »whirlwind.«

THE VALUE OF TRUTHFUL THINKING

I. **Thought contains a vital principle**, because it is the creative principle of the Universe and by its nature will combine with other similar thoughts.

2. As the one purpose of life is **growth**, all principles underlying existence must contribute to give it effect. Thought, therefore, takes form and the Law of Growth eventually brings it into manifestation.

This happens through the Principle of Correspondence or the more generic 'Law of Attraction'.

3. You may freely choose what you think, but the result of your thought is governed by an **immutable law**. Any line of thought persisted in cannot fail to produce its result in the character, health and circumstances of the individual. Methods whereby we can substitute habits of constructive thinking for those which we have found produce only undesirable effects are therefore of primary importance.

4. We all know that this is by no means easy. Mental habits are difficult to control, but it can be done and the way to do it is to begin at once to substitute constructive thought for destructive thought. **Form the habit of analysing every thought**. If it is necessary, if its manifestation in the objective will be a benefit, not only to yourself, but to all whom it may affect in any way, keep it; treasure it; it is of value; it is in tune with the Infinite; it will grow and develop and produce fruit an hundred fold. On the other hand, it will be well for you to keep this quotation from George Matthew Adams, in mind, »Learn to keep the door shut, keep out of your mind, out of your office, and out of your world, every element that seeks admittance with no definite helpful end in view.«

George Matthew Adams was a newspaper columnist, author, writer, philosopher and publisher who founded the Adams Newspaper Service in 1907. He is the author of several books, and '*You Can*' is the most famous of his works.

5. If your thought has been critical or destructive, and has resulted in any condition of discord or inharmony in your environment, it may be necessary for you to **cultivate a mental attitude** which will be conducive to constructive thought.

6. The imagination will be found to be a great assistance in this direction; the cultivation of the imagination leads to the development of the ideal out of which your future will emerge.

7. The imagination gathers up the material by which the mind weaves the fabric in which your future is to be clothed.

8. Imagination is the light by which we can penetrate new worlds of thought and experience.

9. Imagination is the mighty instrument by which every discoverer, every inventor, opened the way from precedent to experience. Precedent said, »It cannot be done;« experience said, »It is done.«

10. Imagination is a plastic power, moulding the things of sense into new forms and ideals.

11. Imagination is the constructive form of thought which must precede every constructive form of action.

12. A builder cannot build a structure of any kind until he has first received the plans from the architect, and the architect must get them from his imagination.

13. The Captain of Industry cannot build a giant corporation which may coordinate hundreds of smaller corporations and thousands of employees, and utilize millions of dollars of capital until he has first created the entire work in his imagination. Objects in the material world are as clay in the potter's hand; **it is in the Master Mind that the real things are created**, and it is by the use of the imagination that the work is done. In order to cultivate the imagination it must be exercised. **Exercise is necessary** to cultivate mental muscle as well as physical muscle. It must be supplied with nourishment or it cannot grow.

14. Do not confuse Imagination with Fancy, or that form of day dreaming in which some people like to indulge. Day dreaming is a form of mental dissipation which may lead to mental disaster.

15. Constructive imagination means mental labour, by some considered to be the hardest kind of labour, but, if so, it yields the greatest returns, for **all the great things in life have come to men and women who had the capacity to think, to imagine, and to make their dreams come true**.

16. When you have become thoroughly conscious of the fact that mind is the only creative principle, that it is Omnipotent, Omniscient and Omnipresent, and that you can consciously

The recognition and demonstration of knowledge is what constitutes power, and this power is spiritual power.

come into harmony with this Omnipotence through your power of thought, you will have taken a long step in the right direction.

17. The next step is to place yourself in position to receive this power. As it is Omnipresent, **it must be within you**. We know that this is so because we know that all power is from within, but it must be developed, unfolded, cultivated; in order to do this we must be receptive, and this receptivity is acquired just as physical strength is gained, by exercise.

18. The Law of Attraction will certainly and unerringly bring to you the conditions, environment, and experiences in life, corresponding with your habitual, characteristic, predominant mental attitude. Not what you think once in a while when you are in church, or have just read a good book, but **your predominant mental attitude is what counts**.

19. You can not entertain weak, harmful, negative thoughts ten hours a day and expect to bring about beautiful, strong and harmonious conditions by ten minutes of strong, positive, creative thought.

20. Real power comes from within. All power that anybody can possibly use is within man, only waiting to be brought into visibility by his first **recognizing** it, and then **affirming** it as his, **working** it into his consciousness until he **becomes one with it**.

21. People say that they desire abundant life, and so they do, but so many interpret this to mean that if they will exercise their muscles or breathe scientifically, eat certain foods in certain ways, drink so many glasses of water every day of just a certain temperature, keep out of drafts, they will attain the abundant life they seek. The result of such methods is but indifferent. However, when man awakens to the truth, and

That's why he urges us to seek the Silence, to find a quiet spot where we can think, concentrate, visualize and thus form new mental habits.

affirms his oneness with all Life, he finds that he takes on the clear eye, the elastic step, the vigour of youth; he finds that he has discovered the source of all power.

22. **All mistakes are but the mistakes of ignorance**. Knowledge gaining and consequent power is what determines growth and evolution. The recognition and demonstration of knowledge is what constitutes power, and this power is spiritual power, and this spiritual power is the power which lies at the heart of all things; it is the soul of the Universe.

23. This knowledge is the result of man's ability to think; thought is therefore the germ of man's conscious evolution. When man ceases to advance in his thoughts and ideals, his forces immediately begin to disintegrate and his countenance gradually registers these changing conditions.

24. Successful men make it their business to hold ideals of the conditions which they wish to realize. They constantly **hold in mind the next step necessary** to the ideal for which they are striving. Thoughts are the materials with which they build, and the imagination is their mental work-shop. Mind is the ever moving force with which they secure the persons and circumstance necessary to build their success structure, and imagination is the matrix in which all great things are fashioned.

25. If you have been faithful to your ideal, you will hear the call when circumstances are ready to materialize your plans and results will correspond in the exact ratio of your fidelity to your ideal. The ideal steadily held is what predetermines and attracts the necessary conditions for its fulfilment.

26. It is thus that you may weave a garment of spirit and power into the web of your entire existence; it is thus that you may lead a charmed life and be forever protected from all harm; it is thus that you may become a positive force whereby conditions of opulence and harmony may be attracted to you.

27. This is the leaven which is gradually permeating the general consciousness and is largely responsible for the conditions of unrest which are everywhere evident.

28. In the last Part you created a mental image; you brought it from the invisible into the visible; this week I want you to

Remember: Use is the condition under which things come to you. Recognition, affirmation, claim, or Ask, Answer, Receive!

take an object and follow it back to its origination, see of what it really consists. If you do this **you will develop imagination, insight, perception, and sagacity.** These come not by the superficial observation of the multitude, but by **a keen analytical observation which sees below the surface**.

29. **It is the few who know that the things which they see are only effects,** and understand the causes by which these effects were brought into existence.

30. Take the same position as heretofore and visualize a Battleship; see the grim monster floating on the surface of the water; there appears to be no life anywhere about; all is silence; you know that by far the largest part of the vessel is under water; out of sight; you know that the ship is as large and as heavy as a twenty-story skyscraper; you know that there are hundreds of men ready to spring to their appointed task instantly; you know that every department is in charge of able, trained, skilled officials who have proven themselves competent to take charge of this marvellous piece of mechanism; you know that although it lies apparently oblivious to everything else, it has eyes which see everything for miles around, and nothing is permitted to escape its watchful vision; you know that while it appears quiet, submissive and innocent, it is prepared to hurl a steel projectile weighing thousands of pounds at an enemy many miles away; this and much more you can bring to mind with comparatively no effort whatever. But how did the battleship come to be where it is; how did it come into existence in the first place? All of this you want to know if you are a careful observer.

31. Follow the great steel plates through the foundries, see the thousands of men employed in their production; go still further back, and see the ore as it comes from the mine, see it loaded on barges or cars, see it melted and properly treated; go back still further and see the architect and engineers who planned the vessel; let the thought carry you back still further in order to determine why they planned the vessel; you will see that you are now so far back that the vessel is something intangible, it no longer exists, it is now only a thought

This exercise contains some symbolism. Once you have mastered the skill of tracing a material object back to its spiritual origin, dwell a moment on the thought that the battleship is your body, and the *"hundreds of men ready to spring to their appointed task instantly"* are the cells, each with their own consciousness and intelligence – and thought - or You! - being the Commander-in-chief!

111

existing in the brain of the architect; but from where did the order come to plan the vessel? Probably from the Secretary of Defence; but probably this vessel was planned long before the war was thought of, and that Congress had to pass a bill appropriating the money; possibly there was opposition, and speeches for or against the bill. Whom do these Congressmen represent? **They represent you and me**, so that our line of thought begins with the Battleship and ends with ourselves, and we find in the last analysis that **our own thought is responsible for this and many other things, of which we seldom think**, and a little further reflection will develop the most important fact of all and that is, if someone had not discovered the law by which this tremendous mass of steel and iron could be made to float upon the water, instead of immediately going to the bottom, the battleship could not have come into existence at all.

32. This law is that, »the specific gravity of any substance is the weight of any volume of it, compared with an equal volume of water.« The discovery of this law revolutionized every kind of ocean travel, commerce and warfare, and made the existence of the battleship, aircraft carriers, and cruise ships possible.

33. You will find exercises of this kind invaluable. When the thought has been trained to look below the surface, everything takes on a different appearance. The insignificant becomes significant, the uninteresting interesting; the things which we supposed to be of no importance are seen to be the only really vital things in existence.

Look To This Day For it is Life, the very Life of Life. In its brief course lie all the Verities and Realities of your existence; The Bliss of Growth; The Glory of Action; The Splendour of Beauty; For Yesterday is but a Dream, And tomorrow is only a Vision; But Today well lived makes every Yesterday a Dream of Happiness, and Every Tomorrow a Vision of Hope. Look well, therefore, to This Day!
— FROM THE SANSKRIT

71. *What is the imagination?*
A form of constructive thought. The light by which we penetrate new worlds of thought and experience. The mighty instrument by which every inventor or discoverer opened the way from precedent to experience.

72. *What is the result of imagination?*
The cultivation of the imagination leads to the development of the ideal out of which your future will emerge.

73. *How may it be cultivated?*
By exercise; it must be supplied with nourishment or it cannot live.

74. *How does imagination differ from day dreaming?*
Day dreaming is a form of mental dissipation, while imagination is a form of constructive thought which must precede every constructive action.

75. *What are mistakes?*
The result of ignorance.

76. *What is knowledge?*
The result of man's ability to think.

77. *What is the power with which successful men build?*
Mind is the very moving force with which they secure the persons and circumstances necessary to complete their plans.

78. *What pre-determines the result?*
The ideal held steadily in mind attracts the necessary conditions for its fulfilment.

79. *What is the result of a keen analytical observation?*
The development of imagination, insight, perception and sagacity.

80. *To what do these lead?*
Opulence and harmony.

114

9

ACT AS THE BLOSSOM OF THOUGHT

PART NINE

In this Part you may learn to fashion the tools by which you may build for yourself any condition you desire.

If you wish to change conditions **you must change yourself**. Your whims, your wishes, your fancies, your ambitions may be thwarted at every step, but your inmost thoughts will find expression just as certainly as the plant springs from the seed.

Suppose, then, we desire to change conditions, how are we to bring this about? The reply is simple: By the Law of Growth. Cause and effect are as absolute and undeviating in the hidden realm of thought as in the world of material things.

Hold in mind the condition desired; **affirm it as an already existing fact**. This indicates the value of a powerful affirmation. By constant repetition it becomes a part of ourselves. We are actually changing ourselves; are making ourselves what we want to be.

Character is not a thing of chance, but it is the result of **continued effort**. If you are timid, vacillating, self-conscious, or if you are over-anxious or harassed by thoughts of fear or impending danger, remember that is axiomatic that »**two things cannot exist in the same place at the same time**.« Exactly the same thing is true in the mental and spiritual world; so that your remedy is plainly to substitute thoughts of courage, power, self-reliance and confidence, for those of fear, lack and limitation.

The easiest and most natural way to do this is to select an affirmation which seems to fit your particular case. The positive thought will destroy the negative as certainly as light destroys darkness, and the results will be just as effectual.

Act is the blossom of thought, and conditions are the result of action, so that you constantly have in your possession the tools by which you will certainly and inevitably make or unmake yourself, and joy or suffering will be the reward.

ACT AS THE BLOSSOM OF THOUGHT

1. There are only three things which can possibly be desired in the »world without« and each of them can be found in the »world within.« The secret of finding them is simply to apply

PLEASE NOTE: All of your affirmations need to be in the "I AM" form, the present tense, for this indicates fulfilment and oneness rather than lack and separation. Thoughts respond to like thoughts, and the faith or belief that "I AM" will ultimately lead to the knowledge of "I AM".

116

the proper »mechanism« of attachment to the omnipotent power to which each individual has access.

2. The three things which all mankind desires and which are necessary for his highest expression and complete development are Health, Wealth and Love. All will admit that **Health** is absolutely essential; no one can be happy if the physical body is in pain. All will not so readily admit that **Wealth** is necessary, but all must admit that a sufficient supply at least is necessary, and what would be considered sufficient for one, would be considered absolute and painful lack for another; and as Nature provides not only enough but abundantly, wastefully, lavishly, we realize that any lack or limitation is only the limitation which has been made by an artificial method of distribution.

3. All will probably admit that **Love** is the third, or maybe some will say the first essential necessary to the happiness of mankind; at any rate, those who possess all three, Health, Wealth, and Love, find nothing else which can be added to their cup of happiness.

4. We have found that the Universal Substance is »All Health,« »All Substance« and »All Love« and that the mechanism of attachment whereby we can consciously connect with this Infinite supply is in our method of thinking. To think correctly is therefore to enter into the »**Secret Place of the Most High**.«

Psalms 91:1: "He who dwells in the Secret Place of the Most High shall abide under the shadow of the Almighty."

5. What shall we think? If we know this we shall have found the proper mechanism of attachment which will relate us to »**Whatsoever things we desire.**« This mechanism may seem very simple when I give it to you, but read on; you will find that it is in reality the »Master Key,« the »Aladdin's lamp,« if you please; you will find that it is the foundation, the imperative condition, the absolute law of well-doing, which means ‚well-being.

This is a reference to Mark, 11:24. The full quote and its meaning is explained in Part 11.

6. To think correctly, accurately, we must know the »Truth.« **The truth then is the underlying principle in every business or social relation**. It is a condition precedent to every right action. To know the truth, to be **sure**, to be **confident**, affords

a satisfaction beside which no other is at all comparable; it is the only solid ground in a world of doubt, conflict and danger.

7. To know the Truth is to be in harmony with the Infinite and Omnipotent power. To know the truth is, therefore, to connect yourself with a power which is irresistible and which will sweep away every kind of discord, inharmony, doubt or error of any kind, because the »Truth is mighty and will prevail.«

8. The humblest intellect can readily foretell the result of any action when he knows that it is based on truth, but the mightiest intellect, the most profound and penetrating mind loses its way hopelessly and can form no conception of the results which may ensue when his hopes are based on a premise which he knows to be false.

9. Every action which is not in harmony with Truth, whether through ignorance or design, will result in discord, and eventual loss in proportion to its extent and character.

10. How then are we to know the truth in order to attach this mechanism which will relate us to the Infinite?

A vital principle: that which ensures and facilitates continuation of life.

11. We can make no mistake about this if we realize that **truth is the vital principle of the Universal Mind** and is Omnipresent. For instance, if you require health, a realization of the fact that **the »I« in you is spiritual** and that **all spirit is one**; that wherever a part is the whole must be, will bring about a condition of health, because every cell in the body must manifest the truth as you see it. If you see sickness; they will manifest sickness; if you see perfection they must manifest perfection. The affirmation »*I am whole, perfect, strong, powerful, loving, harmonious and happy*« will bring about harmonious conditions. The reason for this is because the affirmation is in strict accordance with the Truth, and when truth appears every form of error or discord must necessarily disappear.

This is the Master Key! Please reread this point and meditate over it until you have fully grasped its meaning. Remember how the Conscious Mind acts on the Subconscious Mind and how we can rely on its operation. However, repeating this affirmation is only one element, the other ones being visualization (see below) and action, as soon as the right opportunity arises. An affirmation is a great start, but on its own will not accomplish anything.

12. You have found that the »I« is spiritual, it must necessarily then always be no less than perfect. The affirmation »*I am whole, perfect, strong, powerful, loving, harmonious and happy*« is therefore an exact scientific statement.

13. Thought is a spiritual activity and spirit is creative, therefore the result of holding this thought in mind must necessarily bring about conditions in harmony with the thought.

14. If you require wealth, a realization of the fact that the »I« in you is one with the Universal Mind which is all substance, and is omnipotent, will assist you in bringing into operation the Law of Attraction. This will bring you into vibration with those forces which make for success and bring about conditions of power and affluence in direct proportion with the character and purpose of your affirmation.

15. Visualization is the mechanism of the attachment which you require. Visualization is a very different process from seeing; seeing is physical, and is therefore related to the objective world, the »world without,« but visualization is a product of the imagination, and is therefore a product of the Subjective Mind, the »world within.« It therefore possesses **vitality**; it will grow. **The thing visualized will manifest itself in form**. The mechanism is perfect; it was created by the Master Architect who »doth all things well,« but unfortunately sometimes the operator is inexperienced or inefficient, but **practice and determination** will overcome this defect.

16. If you require Love try to realize that the only way to get love is by giving it, and that **the more you give the more you will get**. The only way in which you can give it, is to fill yourself with it, until you become a magnet. The method was explained in another lesson.

17. He who has learned to bring the greatest spiritual truths into touch with the so-called lesser things of life has discovered the secret of the solution of his problem. One is always quickened, made more thoughtful, by this nearness of approach to great ideas, great events, great natural objects, and great men. Lincoln is said to have begotten in all who came near him the feeling awakened when one approaches a mountain, and this sense asserts itself most keenly when one comes to realize that he has laid hold upon things that are eternal, the power of Truth.

18. It is sometimes an inspiration to hear from someone who has actually put these principles to the test, someone who has

demonstrated them in their own life. A letter from Frederick Andrews offers the following insight:
"Dear Friend:

You will find my experience published in the March issue of '*Nautilus*,' and you are at liberty to make any extracts from or reference to it that may suit your purpose.

Sincerely yours,
Frederick Andrews,
512 Odd Fellows Building,
Indianapolis, Ind."

In September 1917 Frederick Elias Andrews also gave a talk on this subject at the Third Congress of the International New Thought Alliance in St. Louis, Missouri, titled: "*How I gained Health*".

19. I was about thirteen years old when Dr. T. W. Marsee, since passed over, said to my mother: »There is no possible chance, Mrs. Andrews. I lost my little boy the same way, after doing everything for him that it was possible to do. I have made a special study of these cases, and I know there is no possible chance for him to get well.«

20. She turned to him and said: »Doctor, what would you do if he were your boy?« And he answered, »I would fight, fight as long as there is a breath of life to fight for.«

21. That was the beginning of a long drawn-out battle, with many ups and downs, the doctors all agreeing that there was no chance for a cure, though they encouraged and cheered us the best they could.

22. But at last the victory came, and I have grown from a little, crooked, twisted, cripple, going about on my hands and knees, to a strong, straight, well formed man.

23. Now, I know you want the formula, and I will give it to you as briefly and quickly as I can.

24. I built up an affirmation for myself, taking the qualities I most needed, and affirming for myself over and over again, »***I am whole, perfect, strong, powerful, loving, harmonious and happy.***« I kept up this affirmation, always the same, never varying, till I could wake up in the night and find myself repeating, »***I am whole, perfect, strong, powerful,***

Charles Haanel eventually extended this affirmation by F. E. Andrews in "*A Book about YOU*" by inserting "wealthy" in front of the "happy", although with those seven attributes you cannot but be wealthy.

120

Whatever you desire for yourself, affirm it for others, and it will help you both.

loving, harmonious and happy. « It was the last thing on my lips at night and the first thing in the morning.

25. Not only did I affirm it for myself, but for others that I knew needed it. I want to emphasize this point. **Whatever you desire for yourself, affirm it for others, and it will help you both**. We reap what we sow. If we send out thoughts of love and health, they return to us like bread cast upon the waters; but if we send out thoughts of fear, worry, jealousy, anger, hate, etc. , we will reap the results in our own lives.

26. It used to be said that Man is completely built over every seven years, but some scientists now declare that **we build ourselves over entirely every eleven months**; so we are really only eleven months old. If we build the defects back into our bodies year after year, we have no one to blame but ourselves.

27. Man is the sum total of his own thoughts; so the question is, how are we going to entertain only the good thoughts and reject the evil ones? At first we can't keep the evil thoughts from coming, but we can keep from entertaining them. The only way to do this is to forget them — which means, get something for them. This is where the ready-made affirmation comes into play.

28. When a thought of anger, jealousy, fear or worry creeps in, just start your affirmation going. The way to fight darkness is with light — the way to fight cold is with heat — the way to overcome evils is with good. For myself, I never could find any help in denials. **Affirm the good, and the bad will vanish**.
   – Frederick Elias Andrews

29. If there is anything you require, it will be well for you to make use of this affirmation; it cannot be improved upon. Use it just as it is; take it into the silence with you, until it sinks into your subconsciousness, so that you can use it anywhere, in your

Repetition, repetition, repetition!

There is no other. We're not all the same, but we're all one. And what you give to others, even if only mentally, you essentially give to yourself, too, as it expands your own consciousness.

121

car, in the office, at home; this is the advantage of spiritual methods; they are always available. Spirit is omnipresent, every ready; all that is required is a proper recognition of its omnipotence, and a willingness or desire to become the recipient of its beneficent effects.

30. If our predominant mental attitude is one of power, courage, kindliness and sympathy, we shall find that our environment will reflect conditions in correspondence with these thoughts; if it is weak, critical, envious and destructive, we shall find our environment reflecting conditions corresponding to these thoughts.

31. Thoughts are causes and conditions are effects. Herein is the explanation of the origin of both good and evil. **Thought is creative and will automatically correlate with its object**. This is a cosmological law (a universal law), the Law of Attraction, the Law of Cause and Effect; the recognition and application of this law will determine both beginning and end; it is the law by which in all ages and in all times the people were led to believe in the power of prayer. »As thy faith is, so be it unto thee,« is simply another, shorter and a better way of stating it.

As thought correlates with its object, you can be sure of the effect (the object), once you've consciously set the cause (the thought) in motion.

32. This week visualize a plant; take a flower, the one you most admire, bring it from the unseen into the seen, plant the tiny seed, water it, care for it, place it where it will get the direct rays of the morning sun, see the seed burst; it is now a living thing, something which is alive and beginning to search for the means of subsistence. See the roots penetrating the Earth, watch them shoot out in all directions and remember that they are living cells dividing and subdividing, and that they will soon number millions, that each cell is intelligent, that it knows what is wants and knows how to get it. See the stem shoot forward and upward, watch it burst through the surface of the Earth, see it divide and form branches, see how perfect and symmetrical each branch is formed, see the leaves begin to form, and then the tiny stems, each one holding aloft a bud, and as you watch you see the bud begin to unfold and your favourite flower comes to view; and now if you will concentrate intently you will become conscious of a fragrance; it is

As with the previous exercise, this one also contains symbolism. The seed is your thought, which you plant in your mind and leave it undisturbed. Just as with the plant seed, it needs darkness (Silence & Meditation) to grow roots. Then, and only then, will it reach for the sun (the ideal) with absolute strength and certainty. This is why it is so important that we allow our thoughts to grow in the Silence, too, so that no residual doubt of our own or criticism from the out- side can destroy them. Materializa- tion is subconscious, so once the process has gathered enough life force, it will proceed with invari- able precision until the goal has been reached.

122

the fragrance of the flower as the breeze gently sways the beautiful creation which you have visualized.

33. When you are enabled to make your vision clear and complete **you will be enabled to enter into the spirit of a thing**; it will become very real to you; you will be learning to concentrate and the process is the same, whether you are concentrating on health, a favourite flower, an ideal, a complicated business proposition or any other problem of life.

34. Every success has been accomplished by persistent concentration upon the object in view.

In the end, thought rules the world. There are times when impulses and passions are more powerful, but they soon expend themselves, while Mind, acting constantly, is ever ready to drive them back and work when their energy is exhausted.
— J. MCCOSH

PART NINE — QUESTIONS AND ANSWERS

81. *What is the imperative condition of all well-being?*
     Well doing.

82. *What is the condition precedent to every right action?*
     Right thinking.

83. *What is the underlying condition necessary in
     every business transaction or social relation?*
     To know the Truth.

84. *What is the result of a knowledge of the Truth?*
     We can readily predict the result of any action
     that is based upon a true premise.

85. *What is the result of any action based upon a false premise?*
     We can form no conception of the results which may ensue.

86. *How may we know the Truth?*
     By a realization of the fact that Truth is the vital principle
     of the Universe and is therefore omnipresent.

87. *What is the nature of Truth?*
     It is spiritual.

88. *What is the secret of the solution to every problem?*
     To apply spiritual Truth.

89. *What is the advantage of spiritual methods?*
     They are always available.

90. *What are the necessary requirements?*
     A recognition of the omnipotence of spiritual power and
     a desire to become the recipient of its beneficent effects.

LIFE IN HARMONY WITH NATURAL LAW

If you get a thorough understanding or the thought contained in Part Ten, you will have learned that **nothing happens without a definite cause**. You will be enabled to formulate your plans in accordance with exact knowledge. You will know how to control any situation by bringing adequate causes into play. When you win, as you will, you will know exactly why.

The ordinary man, who has no definite knowledge of cause and effect, is governed by his feelings or emotions. He thinks chiefly to justify his action. If he fails as a businessman, he says that luck is against him. If he dislikes music, he says that music is an expensive luxury. If he is a poor office man, he says that he could succeed better at some outdoor work. If he lacks friends, he says his individuality is too fine to be appreciated.

He never thinks his problem through to the end. In short, he does not know that every effect is the result of a certain definite cause, but he seeks to console himself with explanations and excuses. He thinks only in self-defence.

On the contrary, the man who understands that there is no effect without an adequate cause thinks **impersonally**. He gets down to bed rock facts regardless of consequences. He is free to follow the trail of truth wherever it may lead. He sees the issue clear to the end, and he meets the requirements fully and fairly, and the result is that the world gives him all that it has to give, in friendship, honour, love and approval.

LIFE IN HARMONY WITH NATURAL LAW

1. Abundance is a Natural Law of the Universe. The evidence of this law is conclusive; we see it on every hand. Everywhere Nature is lavish, wasteful, extravagant. **Nowhere is economy observed in any created thing**. Profusion is manifested in everything. The millions and millions of trees and flowers and plants and animals and the vast scheme of reproduction where the process of creating and recreating is forever going on, all indicates the lavishness with which Nature has made provision for Man. That there is an abundance for everyone

is evident, but that many fail to participate in this abundance is also evident; they have not yet come into a realization of the universality of all substance, and that mind is the active principle whereby we are related to the things we desire.

2. **All wealth is the offspring of power**; possessions are of value only as they confer power. Events are significant only as they affect power; all things represent certain forms and degrees of power.

3. Knowledge of cause and effect as shown by the laws governing electricity, chemical affinity and gravitation, enables man to plan courageously and execute fearlessly. These laws are called Natural Laws, because they govern in the physical world, but all power is not physical power; there is also mental power, and there is moral and spiritual power.

4. **Spiritual power is superior because it exists on a higher plane**. It has enabled man to discover the law by which these wonderful forces of Nature could be harnessed and made to do the work of hundreds and thousands of men. It has enabled man to discover laws whereby time and space have been annihilated and the Law of Gravitation to be overcome. The operation of this law is dependent upon spiritual contact, as **Henry Drummond** well says:

5. »In the physical world as we know it, there exists the organic and the inorganic. The inorganic or the mineral world is absolutely cut off from the plant or animal world; the passage is hermetically sealed. These barriers have never yet been crossed. No change of substance, no modification of environment, no chemistry, no electricity, no form of energy, no evolution of any kind can ever endow a single atom of the mineral world with the attribute of Life.

6. »Only by the bending down into this dead world of some living form can those dead atoms be gifted with the properties of vitality; without this contact with life they remain fixed in the inorganic sphere forever. Huxley says that the doctrine of Biogenesis (or life only from life) is victorious all along the line, and Tyndall is compelled to say: ‚I affirm that no shred of trustworthy evidence exists to prove that life in our day has ever appeared independent of antecedent life.‘

Henry Drummond (1851 – 1897)

127

7. »Physical laws may explain the inorganic, Biology explains and accounts for the development of the organic, but of the point of contact Science is silent. A similar passage exists between the Natural world and the Spiritual world; this passage is hermetically sealed on the natural side. The door is closed; no man can open it; no organic change, no mental energy, no moral effort, no progress of any kind can enable any human being to enter the spiritual world.«

8. But as the plant reaches down into the mineral world and touches it with the mystery of Life, so **the Universal Mind reaches down into the human mind** and endows it with new, strange, wonderful and even marvellous qualities. All men or women who have every accomplished anything in the world of industry, commerce or art have accomplished because of this process.

9. **Thought is the connecting link between the Infinite and the finite, between the Universal and the individual**. We have seen that there is an impassable barrier between the organic and the inorganic, and that the only way that matter can unfold is to be impregnated with life; as a seed reaches down into the mineral world and begins to unfold and reach out, the dead matter begins to live, a thousand invisible fingers begin to weave a suitable environment for the new arrival, and as the law of growth begins to take effect, we see the process continue until the Lily finally appears, and even »Solomon in all his glory was not arrayed like one of these«.

10. Even so, a thought is dropped into the invisible substance of the Universal Mind, that substance from which all things are created, and as it takes root, the Law of Growth begins to take effect and we find that conditions and environment are but the objective form of our thought.

...which is being effected through the Principle of Correspondence.

11. The law is that Thought is an active vital form of dynamic energy which has the power to correlate with its object and bring it out of the invisible substance from which all things are created into the visible or objective world. This is the law by which and through which all things come into manifestation; it is the Master Key by which you are admitted into the Secret Place of the Most High and are »given dominion

over all things«. With an understanding of this law you may »**decree a thing and it shall be established unto thee**«.

12. It could not be otherwise; if the soul of the Universe as we know it is the Universal Spirit, then the Universe is simply the condition which the Universal Spirit has made for itself. We are simply individualized spirit and are creating the conditions for our growth in exactly the same way.

13. This creative power depends upon our **recognition** of the potential power of spirit or mind and must not be confused with Evolution. **Creation is the calling into existence of that which does not exist in the objective world**. Evolution is simply the unfolding of potentialities involved in things which already exist.

14. In taking advantage of the wonderful possibilities opened up to us through the operation of this law, we must remember that we ourselves contribute nothing to its efficacy as the Great Teacher said: »It is not I that doth the works, but the Father that dwelleth in me, He doth the work«. We must take exactly the same position; we can do nothing to assist in the manifestation, **we simply comply with the law**, and the All-originating Mind will bring about the result.

He is referring to Jesus, the Christ, here. (Jesus, the Man, who was in possession of a Christ Consciousness.)

15. The great error of the present day is the idea that Man has to originate the intelligence whereby the Infinite can proceed to bring about a specific purpose or result. Nothing of this kind is necessary; the Universal Mind can be depended upon to find the ways and means for bringing about any necessary manifestation. We must, however, create the ideal, and this ideal should be perfect.

It will take time, dedication and practice to create perfect ideals. The subject is being dealt with in detail in a later chapter.

16. We know that the laws governing electricity have been formulated in such a way that this invisible power can be controlled and used for our benefit and comfort in thousands of ways. We know that messages are carried around the world, that ponderous machinery does its bidding, that it now illuminates practically the whole world, but we know too that if we consciously or ignorantly violate its law by touching a live wire, when it is not properly insulated, the result will be unpleasant and possibly disastrous. A lack of understanding

Constructive thought must necessarily be creative,
but creative thought must be harmonious,
and this eliminates all destructive or competitive thought.

of the laws governing in the invisible world has the same result, and many are suffering the consequences all the time.

17. It has been explained that the Law of Causation depends upon polarity – a circuit must be formed. This circuit cannot be formed unless we operate in harmony with the law. How shall we operate in harmony with the law unless we know what the law is? How shall we know what the Law is? **By study, by observation**.

18. We see the law in operation everywhere; all nature testifies to the operation of the law by silently, constantly expressing itself in the Law of Growth. Where there is growth, there must be life; where there is life there must be harmony, so that **everything that has life is constantly attracting to itself the conditions and the supply which is necessary for its most complete expression**.

... and the affirmation "I am whole, perfect, strong, powerful, loving, harmonious and happy!", often repeated and turned into a habit, will result in corresponding words and actions and therefore corresponding effects in the outside world. Always from the spiritual to the material, never the other around.

19. If your thought is in harmony with the creative Principle of Nature, it is in tune with the Infinite Mind, and it will form the circuit, it will not return to you void; but it is possible for you to think thoughts that are not in tune with the Infinite, and when there is no polarity, the circuit is not formed. What, then, is the result? What is the result when a dynamo is generating electricity, the circuit is cut off and there is no outlet? The dynamo stops.

The isolation also leads to resistance, and this eventually leads to blockages on the mental, emotional and physical plane.

20. It will be exactly the same with you, if you entertain thoughts which are not in accordance with the Infinite and cannot therefore be polarized; there is no circuit, you are **isolated**, the thoughts cling to you, harass you, worry you, and finally bring about disease and possibly death; the physician may not diagnose the case exactly in this way, he may give it some fancy name which has been manufactured for the various ills

which are the result of wrong thinking, but the cause is the same nevertheless.

21. Constructive thought must necessarily be creative, but creative thought must be harmonious, and this eliminates all destructive or competitive thought.

22. Wisdom, strength, courage and all harmonious conditions are the result of power and we have seen that all power is from within; likewise, every lack, limitation or adverse circumstance is the result of weakness, and weakness is simply absence of power; it comes from nowhere, it is nothing — the remedy then is simply to **develop power**, and this is accomplished in exactly the same manner that all power is developed, by exercise.

23. This exercise consists in making an application of your knowledge. Knowledge will not apply itself. You must make the application. Abundance will not come to you out of the sky, neither will it drop into your lap, but a conscious realization of the Law of Attraction and the intention to bring it into operation for a certain, definite and specific purpose, and the will to carry out this purpose will bring about the materialization of your desire by a natural law of transference. If you are in business, it will increase and develop along regular channels, possibly new or unusual channels of distribution will be opened and when the law becomes fully operative, you will find **that the things you seek are seeking you**.

24. This week select a blank space on the wall, or any other convenient spot, from where you usually sit, mentally draw a black horizontal line about six inches long, try to see the line as plainly as though it were painted on the wall; now mentally draw two vertical lines connecting with this horizontal line at either end; now draw another horizontal line connecting with the two vertical lines; now you have a **square**. Try to see the square perfectly; when you can do so draw a **circle** within the square; now place a **point** in the centre of the circle; now draw the point toward you about 10 inches; now you have a **cone** on a square base; you will remember that your work was all in black; change it to white, to red, to yellow.

This exercise is highly symbolic. The line is the first "movement" a point (the sponsoring thought) can make. The square (male, symbol of form and structure) "squares" the circle (female, symbol of the Infinite) – which is an old Masonic expression – expressing the Infinite through form and structure.
The point in the circle is the Individual within Infinity (also the symbol of the Sun).
The mental pulling of the dot closer to you is the vortex-shaped attraction into your life of what you are concentrating on, as well as a 3rd dimensional change of degree between you and the Infinite – an approach of the former to the latter with the aim of new conscious co-creation.

25. If you can do this, you are making excellent progress and will soon be enabled to concentrate on any problem you may have in mind.

Please reread this quote by Emerson while keeping the exercise of this part in mind.

"A vivid thought brings the power to paint it; and in proportion to the depth of its source is the force of its projection."
— RALPH WALDO EMERSON

91. *What is Wealth?*
     Wealth is the offspring of power.

92. *Of what value are possessions?*
     Possessions are of value only as they confer power.

93. *Of what value is a knowledge of cause and effect?*
     It enables men to plan courageously and execute fearlessly.

94. *How does life originate in the inorganic world?*
     Only by the introduction of some living
     form. There is no other way.

95. *What is the connecting link between
     the Finite and the Infinite?*
     Thought is the connecting link.

96. *Why is that so?*
     Because the Universal can manifest
     only through the individual.

97. *Upon what does causation depend?*
     Upon polarity; a circuit must be formed; the Universal
     is the positive side of the battery of life, the individual
     is the negative, and thought forms the circuit.

98. *Why do many fail to secure harmonious conditions?*
     They do not understand the law; there is no
     polarity; they have not formed the circuit.

99. *What is the remedy?*
     A conscious recognition of the Law of
     Attraction with the intention of bringing it
     into existence for a definite purpose.

100. *What will be the result?*
     Thought will correlate with its object and bring it into
     manifestation, because thought is a product of the spiritual
     Man, and spirit is the creative principle of the Universe.

133

INDUCTIVE REASONING

Your life is governed by law – by actual, immutable principles that never vary. **Law is in operation at all times; in all places**. Fixed laws underlie all human actions. For this reason, men who control giant industries are enabled to determine with absolute precision just what percentage of every hundred thousand people will respond to any given set of conditions.

It is well, however, to remember that while every effect is the result of a cause, **the effect in turn becomes a cause**, which creates other effects, which in turn create still other causes; so that when you put the Law of Attraction into operation you must remember that you are **starting a train of causation** for good or otherwise which may have endless possibilities.

We frequently hear it said, »A very distressing situation came into my life, which could not have been the result of my thought, as I certainly never entertained any thought which could have such a result«. We fail to remember that like attracts like in the mental world, and that the thought which we entertain brings to us certain friendships, companionships of a particular kind, and these in turn bring about conditions and environment, which in turn are responsible for the conditions of which we complain.

INDUCTIVE REASONING

1. Inductive reasoning is the process of the Subjective Mind by which we compare a number of separate instances with one another until we see the common factor that gives rise to them all.
2. Induction proceeds by comparison of facts; it is this method of studying nature which has resulted in the discovery of a reign of law which has marked an epoch in human progress.
3. It is the dividing line between superstition and intelligence; it has eliminated the elements of uncertainty and caprice from men's lives and substituted law, reason, and certitude.
4. It is the »Watchman at the Gate« mentioned in a former lesson.
5. When, by virtue of this principle, the world to which the senses were accustomed had been revolutionized; when the

Be quiet, observe the thoughts that try to gain access to your Conscious Mind, and allow only those entry that are in harmony with the Universal Mind – that close the circuit!

136

Sun had been arrested in his course, the apparently flat Earth had been shaped into a ball and set whirling around it; when the inert matter had been resolved into active elements, and the Universe presented itself wherever we directed the telescope and microscope, full of force, motion and life, we are constrained to ask by what possible means the delicate forms of organization in the midst of it are kept in order and repair.

6. Like poles and like forces repel themselves or remain impenetrable to each other, and this cause seems in general sufficient to assign a proper place and distance to stars, men and forces. As men of different virtues enter into partnership, so do opposite poles attract each other, elements that have no property in common like acids and gases cling to each other in preference and a general exchange is kept up between the surplus and the demand.

7. As the eye seeks and receives satisfaction from colours complementary to those which are given, so does need, want and desire, in the largest sense, induce, guide and determine action.

8. It is our privilege to become conscious of the principle and act in accordance with it. **Georges Cuvier** sees a tooth belonging to an extinct race of animals. This tooth wants a body for the performance of its function, and it defines the peculiar body it stands in need of with such precision that Cuvier is able to reconstruct the frame of this animal.

Georges Cuvier (1769 – 1832)

9. Perturbations are observed in the motion of Uranus. **Urbain Le Verrier** needs another star at a certain place to keep the solar system in order, and Neptune appears in the place and hour appointed.

10. The instinctive wants of the animal and the intellectual wants of Cuvier, the wants of nature and of the mind of Le Verrier were alike, and thus the results; here the thoughts of an existence, there an existence. A well-defined lawful want, therefore, furnishes the reason for the more complex operations of nature.

Urbain Le Verrier (1811 – 1877)

137

11. Having recorded correctly the answers furnished by nature and stretched our senses with the growing science over her surface; having joined hands with the levers that move the Earth, we become conscious of such a close, varied and deep contact with the world without, that our wants and purposes become no less identified with the harmonious operations of this vast organization, than the life, liberty, and happiness of the citizen is identified with the existence of his government.

12. As the interests of the individual are protected by the arms of the country, added to his own, and his needs may depend upon certain supply in the degree that they are felt more universally and steadily, in the same manner does conscious citizenship in the Republic of Nature secure us from the annoyances of subordinate agents by alliance with superior powers; and by appeal to the fundamental laws of resistance or inducement offered to mechanical or chemical agents, distribute the labour to be performed between them and Man to the best advantage of the inventor.

13. If **Plato** could have witnessed the pictures taken of the Sun with the assistance of the photographer, or a hundred similar illustrations of what Man does by induction, he would perhaps have been reminded of the intellectual midwifery of his master, and in his own mind might have arisen the vision of a land where all manual, mechanical labour and repetition is assigned to the power of nature, where our wants are satisfied by purely mental operations set in motion by the will, and where the supply is created by the demand.

Plato (428/427 BC – 348/347 BC)

14. However distant that land may appear, induction has taught men to make strides toward it and has surrounded him with benefits which are, at the same time, rewards for past fidelity, and incentives for more assiduous devotion.

15. It is also an aid in concentrating and strengthening our faculties for the remaining part, giving unerring solution for individual as well as universal problems by the mere operations of mind in the purest form.

16. Here we find a **method**, the spirit of which is **to believe that what is sought has been accomplished**, in order to accomplish it: a method, bequeathed upon us by the same

Plato who, outside of this sphere, could never find how the ideas became realities.

17. This conception is also elaborated by **Swedenborg** in his doctrine of correspondences, and a still greater teacher has said, »*Therefore I say unto you, All things whatsoever ye pray and ask for, believe that ye have received them, and ye shall have them.*« (Mark 11:24) The difference of the tenses in this passage is remarkable.

18. We are first to believe that our desire **has already been fulfilled**, its accomplishment will then follow. This is a concise direction for making use of the creative power of thought by impressing on the Universal, Subjective Mind the particular thing which we desire **as an already existing fact.**

19. **We are thus thinking on the plane of the Absolute** and eliminating all consideration of conditions or limitation and are planting a seed which, if left undisturbed, will finally germinate into external fruition.

20. To review: Inductive reasoning is the process of the Subjective Mind, by which we compare a number of separate instances with one another until we see the common factor that gives rise to them all. We see people in every civilized country on the globe, securing results by some process which they do not seem to understand themselves, and to which they usually attach more or less mystery. Our reason is given to us for the purpose of ascertaining the law by which these results are accomplished.

21. The operation of this thought process is seen in those fortunate natures that possess everything that others must acquire by toil, who never have a struggle with conscience because they always act correctly, and can never conduct themselves otherwise than with tact, learn everything easily, complete everything they begin with a happy knack, live in eternal harmony with themselves, without ever reflecting much what they do, or ever experiencing difficulty or toil.

22. The fruit of this thought is, as it were, **a gift of the gods**, but a gift which few as yet realize, appreciate, or understand. The recognition of the marvellous power which is possessed by

Emanuel Swedenborg (1688 – 1772)

As with everything in the Bible, there are several translations available for Mark 11:24. Here I chose the one that still had the old feel to it (English Revised Version), but also placed emphasis on the past tense ("received"), because this is what Charles Haanel refers to in the following sentence.

The "seeing of the thing which we desire as an already existing fact" is the main challenge, as our senses indicate to us things that have their cause set in the past. It is for us to ignore those indications and focus solely on our inner world, on our new, creative thoughts, and there we have to become one with the object of our desire!

the mind under proper conditions and the fact that this power can be utilized, directed, and made available for the solution of every human problem is of transcendental importance.

23. **All truth is the same**, whether stated in modern scientific terms or in the language of apostolic times. There are timid souls who fail to realize that the very completeness of truth requires various statement — that no one human formula will show every side of it.

24. Changing emphasis, new language, novel interpretations, unfamiliar perspectives, are not, as some suppose, signs of departure from truth but on the contrary, they are evidence that the truth is being apprehended in new relations to human needs, and is becoming more generally understood.

25. **The truth must be told to each generation and to every people in new and different terms**, so that when the Great Teacher said — »Believe that ye receive and ye shall receive« or, when Paul said — »Faith is the substance of things hoped for, the evidence of things not seen« or, when modern science says — »The Law of Attraction is the law by which thought correlates with its object«, each statement when subjected to analysis, is found to contain exactly the same truth. The only difference being in the form of presentation.

26. We are standing on the threshold of a new era. The time has arrived when man has learned the secrets of mastery and the way is being prepared for a new social order, more wonderful than anything every heretofore dreamed of. The conflict of modern science with theology, the study of comparative religions, the tremendous power of new social movements, all of these are but clearing the way for the new order. They may have destroyed traditional forms which have become antiquated and impotent, but nothing of value has been lost.

27. A new faith has been born, a faith which demands a new form of expression, and this faith is taking form in a deep consciousness of power which is being manifested in the present spiritual activity found on every hand.

28. **The spirit which sleeps in the mineral, breathes in the vegetable, moves in the animal and reaches its highest development in Man is the Universal Mind,**

We are thinking on the plane of the absolute and eliminating all consideration of conditions or limitation. We are planting a seed which, if left undisturbed, will finally germinate into external fruition.

and it behooves us to span the gulf between being and doing, theory and practice, by demonstrating our understanding of the dominion which we have been given.

29. By far the greatest discovery of all the centuries is the power of thought. The importance of this discovery has been a little slow in reaching the general consciousness, but it has arrived, and already in every field of research the importance of this greatest of all great discoveries is being demonstrated.

30. You ask, in what does the creative power of thought consist? It consists in **creating ideas**, and these in turn objectify themselves by **appropriating, inventing, observing, discerning, discovering, analysing, ruling, governing, combining, and applying matter and force**. It can do this because it is an intelligent creative power.

31. Thought reaches its loftiest activity when plunged into its own mysterious depth; when it breaks through the narrow compass of self and passes from truth to truth to the region of eternal light, where all which is, was or ever will be, melt into one grand harmony.

32. From this process of self-contemplation comes inspiration which is creative intelligence, and which is undeniably superior to every element, force or law of nature, because it can **understand, modify, govern and apply them** to its own ends and purposes and therefore possess them.

33. Wisdom begins with the dawn of reason, and **reason is but an understanding of the knowledge and principles** whereby we may know the true meaning of things. Wisdom, then, is illuminated reason, and this wisdom leads to humility, for humility is a large part of Wisdom.

34. We all know many who have achieved the seemingly impossible, who have realized life-long dreams, who have changed

everything including themselves. We have sometimes marvelled at the demonstration of an apparently irresistible power, which seemed to be ever available just when it was most needed, but it is all clear now. All that is required is **an understanding of certain definite fundamental principles and their proper application**.

35. For your exercise this week, concentrate on the quotation taken from the Bible, »*Whatsoever ye pray and ask for, believe that ye have received them, and ye shall have them.*«; notice that there is **no limitation**, »Whatsoever« is very definite and implies that the only limitation which is placed upon us is our ability to think, to be equal to the occasion, to rise to the emergency, to remember that Faith is not a shadow, but a substance, »the substance of things hoped for, the evidence of things not seen«.

"Death is but the natural process whereby all material forms are thrown into the crucible for reproduction in fresh diversity."

101. *What is inductive reasoning?*
The process of the Subjective Mind by which we compare
a number of separate instances with each other until we
see the common factor which gives rise to them all.

102. *What has this method of studying accomplished?*
It has resulted in the discovery of a reign of law
which has marked an epoch in human progress.

103. *What is it that guides and determines action?*
It is need, want and desire which in the largest
sense induce, guide and determine action.

104. *What is the formula for the unerring
solution of every individual problem?*
We are to believe that our desire has already been
fulfilled; its accomplishment will then follow.

105. *What great Teachers advocated it?*
Jesus, Plato, Swedenborg.

106. *What is the result of this thought process?*
We are thinking on the plane of the absolute
and planting a seed, which – if left undisturbed
– will germinate into fruition.

107. *Why is it scientifically exact?*
Because it is Natural Law.

108. *What is Faith?*
»Faith is the substance of things hoped
for, the evidence of things unseen.«

109. *What is the Law of Attraction?*
The Law by which Faith is brought into manifestation.

110. *What importance do you attach to an
understanding of this law?*
It has eliminated the elements of uncertainty and caprice
from men's lives and substituted law, reason, and certitude.

UNDERSTANDING THE SPIRITUAL NATURE OF THOUGHT

PART TWELVE

Part Twelve is enclosed herewith. In the fourth paragraph you will find the following statement: »You must first have the knowledge of your power; second, the courage to dare; third, the faith to do.«

If you concentrate upon the thoughts given, if you give them your entire attention, you will find **a world of meaning in each sentence**, and will attract to yourself other thoughts in harmony with them, and you will soon grasp the full significance of the vital knowledge upon which you are concentrating.

Knowledge does not apply itself; we as individuals must make the application, and the application consists in fertilizing the thought with a living purpose.

The time and thought which most persons waste in aimless effort would accomplish wonders if properly directed with some special object in view. In order to do this, it is necessary to centre your mental force upon a specific thought and hold it there, **to the exclusion of all other thoughts**. If you have ever looked through the viewfinder on a camera, you found that when the object was not in focus, the impression was indistinct and possibly blurred, but when the proper focus was obtained the picture was clear and distinct. This illustrates the power of concentration. Unless you can concentrate upon the object which you have in view, you will have but a hazy, indifferent, vague, indistinct and blurred outline of your ideal and the results will be in accordance with your mental picture.

UNDERSTANDING THE SPIRITUAL NATURE OF THOUGHT

1. There is no purpose in life that cannot be best accomplished through a scientific understanding of the creative power of thought.
2. This power to think is common to all. Man is, because he thinks. Man's power to think is infinite, consequently his creative power is unlimited.
3. We know that thought is building for us the thing we think of and actually bringing it nearer, yet we find it difficult to banish fear, anxiety or discouragement, all of which are

Nowhere is written what and how you have to think. If you don't do your own thinking, someone else will do it for you, and what you receive then is what that person or institution wanted, and with which you may agree or not! Make sure your Gatekeeper is always at work, not allowing anything inharmonious to enter your Conscious Mind. Discard it right at the door and concentrate only on desirable things!

146

powerful thought forces, and which continually send the things we desire further away, so that it is often one step forward and two steps backward.

4. The only way to keep from going backward is to keep going forward. **Eternal vigilance is the price of success**. There are three steps, and each one is absolutely essential. **You must first have the knowledge of your power; second, the courage to dare; third, the faith to do**.

5. With this as a basis you can construct an ideal business, an ideal home, ideal friends, and an ideal environment. You are not restricted as to material or cost. Thought is omnipotent and has the power to draw on the Infinite bank of primary substance for all that it requires. **Infinite resources are therefore at your command**.

6. But your ideal must be sharp, clear-cut, definite; to have one ideal today, another tomorrow, and a third next week, means to scatter your forces and accomplish nothing; your result will be a meaningless and chaotic combination of wasted material.

7. Unfortunately this is the result which many are securing, and the cause is self-evident. If a sculptor started out with a piece of marble and a chisel and changed his ideal every fifteen minutes, what result could he expect? And why should you expect any different result in moulding the greatest and most plastic of all substances, the only real substance?

8. The result of this indecision and negative thought is often found in the loss of material wealth. Supposed independence which required many years of toil and effort suddenly disappears. **It is often found then that money and property are not independence at all**. On the contrary, the only independence is found to be a practical working knowledge of the creative power of thought.

9. This practical working method cannot come to you until you learn that **the only real power which you can have is the power to adjust yourself to Divine and unchangeable principles**. You cannot change the Infinite, but you can come into an understanding of natural laws. The reward of this understanding is a conscious realization of your ability to adjust your thought faculties with the Universal Thought

which is Omnipresent. Your ability to cooperate with this Omnipotence will indicate the degree of success with which you meet.

10. The power of thought has many counterfeits which are more or less fascinating, but the results are harmful instead of helpful.

11. Of course, worry, fear, and all negative thoughts produce a crop after their kind; those who harbour thoughts of this kind must inevitably reap what they have sown.

12. Again, there are the Phenomena seekers who gormandize on the so-called proofs and demonstration obtained at materializing seances. They throw open their mental doors and soak themselves in the most poisonous currents which can be found in the psychic world. They do not seem to understand that it is the ability to become negative, receptive and passive, and thus drain themselves of all their vital force, which enables them to bring about these vibratory thought forms.

13. There are also the Hindu worshippers, who see in the materializing phenomena which are performed by the so-called adepts, a source of power, forgetting, or never seeming to realize that as soon as the will is withdrawn the forms wither, and the vibratory forces of which they are composed vanish.

14. Telepathy, or thought transference, has received considerable attention, but as it requires a negative mental state on the part of the receiver, the practice is harmful. A thought may be sent with the intention of hearing or seeing, but it will bring the penalty attached to the inversion of the principle involved.

15. In many instances, hypnotism is positively dangerous to the subject as well as the operator. No one familiar with the laws governing in the mental world would think of attempting to dominate the will of another, for by so doing, he will gradually (but surely) divest himself of his own power.

16. All of these perversions have their temporary satisfaction and for some a keen fascination, but there is an infinitely greater fascination in a true understanding of the world of power within, **a power which increases with use**; which is perma-

Negative, receptive and passive all synonymous. If you become negative, you will always get what someone else has thought up for you. The physical equivalent is that of an electron, which gets directed and used by higher powers of organization in order to create something new.

We have come a considerable distance since then. Telepathy is becoming increasingly common-place, and the purpose is for communication rather than just seeing or hearing.

Charles Haanel refers to stage-hypnotism, which was very popular in those days. Modern hypnotherapy supports the client's will, or his desire, to accomplish a particular goal.

nent instead of fleeing; which not only is potent as a remedial agency to bring about the remedy for past error or results of wrong thinking, but is a prophylactic agency protecting us from all manner and form of danger, and finally is an actual creative force with which we can build new conditions and new environment.

17. **The law is that thought will correlate with its object and bring forth in the material world the correspondence of the thing thought or produced in the mental world.** We then discern the absolute necessity of seeing that every thought has the inherent germ of truth in order that the Law of Growth will bring into manifestation good, for good alone can confer any permanent power.

18. The principle which gives the thought the dynamic power to correlate with its object, and therefore to master every adverse human experience, is the **Law of Attraction**, which is another name for **love**. This is an eternal and fundamental principle, inherent in all things, in every system of Philosophy, in every Religion, and in every Science. There is no getting away from the Law of Love. It is feeling that imparts vitality to thought. Feeling is desire, and desire is love. Thought impregnated with love becomes invincible.

19. We find this truth emphasized wherever the power of thought is understood. The Universal Mind is not only Intelligence, but it is substance, and this substance is the attractive force which brings electrons together by the Law of Attraction so that they form atoms. The atoms in turn are brought together by the same law and form molecules. Molecules take objective forms, and so we find that **the Law of Love is the creative force behind every manifestation**, not only of atoms, but of worlds, of the Universe, of everything of which the imagination can form any conception.

20. It is the operation of this marvellous Law of Attraction which has caused men in all ages and all times to believe that there must be some personal being who responded to their petitions and desires, and manipulated events in order to comply with their requirements.

It is feeling that imparts vitality to thought. Feeling is desire, and desire is love. Thought impregnated with love becomes invincible.

21. It is the combination of Thought and Love which forms the irresistible force, called the Law of Attraction. All natural laws are irresistible, the Law of Gravitation, or electricity, or any other law operates with mathematical exactitude. **There is no variation**, it is only the channel of distribution which may be imperfect. If a bridge falls, we do not attribute the collapse to any variation of the law of gravitation. If a light fails us, we do not conclude that the laws governing electricity cannot be depended upon, and if the Law of Attraction seems to be imperfectly demonstrated by an inexperienced or uninformed person, we are not to conclude that the greatest and most infallible law upon which the entire system of creation depends has been suspended. We should rather conclude that a little more understanding of the law is required, for the same reason that a correct solution of a difficult problem in Mathematics is not always readily and easily obtained.

22. Things are created in the mental or spiritual world before they appear in the outward act or event. By the simple process of governing our thought forces today, we help create the events which will come into our lives in the future, perhaps even tomorrow. **Educated desire is the most potent means of bringing into action the Law of Attraction**.

23. Man is so constituted that he must first create the tools, or implements, by which he gains the power to think. The mind cannot comprehend an entirely new idea until a corresponding vibratory brain cell has been prepared to receive it. This explains why it is so difficult for us to receive or appreciate an entirely new idea; we have no brain cell capable of receiving it; we are therefore incredulous; we do not believe it.

24. If, therefore, you have not been familiar with the omnipotence of the Law of Attraction, and the scientific method by which it can be put into operation, or if you have not been

familiar with the unlimited possibilities which it opens to those who are enabled to take advantage of the resources it offers, **begin now and create the necessary brain cells** which will enable you to comprehend the unlimited powers which may be yours by cooperating with Natural Law. **This is done by concentration or attention**.

25. The intention governs the attention. Power comes through repose. **It is by concentration that deep thoughts, wise speech, and all forces of high potentiality are accomplished**.

26. It is in the Silence that you get into touch with the omnipotent power of the Subconscious Mind, from which all power is evolved.

27. He, who desires wisdom, power, or permanent success of any kind, will find it only within; it is an unfoldment. The unthinking may conclude that the Silence is very simple and easily attained, but it should be remembered that only in absolute Silence may one come into contact with Divinity itself; may learn of the unchangeable law and open for himself the channels by which persistent practice and concentration lead to perfection.

28. This week go to the same room, take the same chair, the same position as previously; be sure to relax, let go, both mentally and physically; always do this; never try to do any mental work under pressure; see that there are no tense muscles or nerves, that you are entirely comfortable. Now realize your unity with Omnipotence; get into touch with this power; come into a deep and vital understanding, appreciation, and realization of the fact that your ability to think is your ability to act upon the Universal Mind, and bring it into manifestation. Realize that it will meet any and every requirement; that you have exactly the same potential ability which any individual ever did have or ever will have, because each is but an expres-

He, who desires wisdom, power, or permanent success of any kind, will find it only within.

151

sion or manifestation of the One. **All are parts of the whole**, there is no difference in kind or quality, the only difference being one of degree.

"Thought cannot conceive of anything that may not be brought to expression. He who first uttered it may be only the suggester, but the doer will appear."
— WILSON

III. *How may any purpose in life be best accomplished?*
Through a scientific understanding of
the spiritual nature of thought.

112. *What three steps are absolutely essential?*
The knowledge of our power, the
courage to dare, the faith to do.

113. *How is the practical working knowledge secured?*
By an understanding of natural laws.

114. *What is the reward of an understanding of these laws?*
A conscious realization of our ability to adjust
ourselves to Divine and unchanging principle.

115. *What will indicate the degree of success with which we meet?*
The degree in which we realize that we cannot
change the Infinite but must cooperate with it.

116. *What is the principle which gives thought its
dynamic power?*
The Law of Attraction which rests on vibration,
which in turn rests upon the law of love. Thought
impregnated with love becomes invincible.

117. *Why is this law irresistible?*
Because it is a Natural Law. All natural laws are
irresistible and unchangeable and act with mathematical
exactitude. There is no deviation or variation.

118. *Why then does it sometimes seem to be difficult
to find the solution to our problems in life?*
For the same reason that it is sometimes difficult to
find the correct solution to a difficult mathematical
problem. The operator is uninformed or inexperienced.

119. *Why is it impossible for the mind to grasp an entirely
new idea?*
We have no corresponding vibratory brain
cell capable of receiving the idea.

120. *How is wisdom secured?*
By concentration; it is an unfoldment; it comes
from within.

THE LAW OF CAUSE AND EFFECT

Physical science is responsible for the marvellous age of invention in which we are now living, but spiritual science is now setting out on a career whose possibilities no one can foretell.

Spiritual science has previously been the football of the uneducated, the superstitious, the mystical, but men are now interested in **definite methods and demonstrated facts only**.

We have come to know that thinking is a spiritual process, that vision and imagination preceded action and event, that the day of the dreamer has come. The following lines by Mr. Herbert Kaufman are interesting in this connection.

»*They are the architects of greatness, their vision lies within their souls, they peer beyond the veils and mists of doubt and pierce the walls of unborn Time. The belted wheel, the trail of steel, the churning screw, are shuttles in the loom on which they weave their magic tapestries. Makers of Empire, they have fought for bigger things than crowns and higher seats than thrones. Your homes are set upon the land a dreamer found. The pictures on its walls are visions from a dreamer's soul.*

They are the chosen few — the blazers of the way. Walls crumble and Empires fall, the tidal wave sweeps from the sea and tears a fortress from its rocks. The rotting nations drop off from Time's bough, and only things the dreamer's make live on.«

Part Thirteen, which follows, tells why the dreams of the dreamer come true. It explains the **Law of Causation** by which dreamers, inventors, authors, financiers, bring about the realization of their desires. It explains the law by which the thing pictured upon our mind eventually becomes our own.

THE LAW OF CAUSE AND EFFECT

I.   It has been the tendency, and, as might be proved, a necessity for science to seek the explanation of everyday facts by a generalization of those others which are less frequent and form the exception. Thus does the eruption of the volcano manifest the heat which is continually at work in the interior of the Earth and to which the latter owes much of her configuration.

A generalization of facts, which are rare, strange, or form the exception, has been the magnetic needle guiding to all the discoveries of inductive science.

2. Thus does the lightning reveal a subtle power constantly busy to produce changes in the inorganic world, and, as dead languages now seldom heard were once ruling among the nations, so does a giant tooth in Siberia, or a fossil in the depth of the Earth, not only bear record of the evolution of past ages, but thereby explains to us the origin of the hills and valleys which we inhabit today.

3. In this way a generalization of facts which are rare, strange, or form the exception, has been the magnetic needle guiding to all the discoveries of inductive science.

4. This method is founded upon reason and experience and thereby destroyed superstition, precedent and conventionality.

5. It is almost three-hundred years since **Lord Bacon** recommended this method of study, to which the civilized nations owe the greater part of their prosperity and the more valuable part of their knowledge; purging the mind from narrow prejudices, denominated theories, more effectually than by the keenest irony; calling the attention of men from heaven to Earth more successfully by surprising experiments than by the most forcible demonstration of their ignorance; educating the inventive faculties more powerfully by the near prospect of useful discoveries thrown open to all, than by talk of bringing to light the innate laws of our mind.

6. The method of Bacon has seized the spirit and aim of the great philosophers of Greece and carried them into effect by the new means of observation which another age offered; thus gradually revealing a wondrous field of knowledge in the infinite space of astronomy, in the microscopic egg of embryology, and the dim age of geology; disclosing an order

Lord Francis Bacon (1561 – 1626)

Once again the mobile phone serves as a simple but practical example of how intention turned into attention, and attention led to consciousness, which then expressed itself in the powerful devices that we are using today. That said, this material device is still nothing compared to your own latent spiritual abilities.

157

of the pulse which the logic of Aristotle could never have unveiled, and analysing into formerly unknown elements the material combinations which no dialectic of the scholastics could force apart.

7. It has lengthened life; it has mitigated pain; it has extinguished diseases; it has increased the fertility of the soil; it has given new securities to the mariner; it has spanned great rivers with bridges of form unknown to our fathers; it has guided the thunderbolt from heaven to Earth; it has lighted up night with the splendour of day; it has extended the range of human vision; it has multiplied the power of the human muscles; it has accelerated motion; it has annihilated distance; it has facilitated intercourse, correspondence, all friendly offices, all dispatch of business; it has enabled men to descend into the depths of the sea, to soar into the air, to penetrate securely into the noxious recesses of the Earth.

8. This then is the true nature and scope of induction. But the greater the success which men have achieved in the inductive science, the more does the whole tenor of their teachings and example impress us with the necessity of **observing carefully, patiently, accurately**, with all the instruments and resources at our command the individual facts before venturing upon a statement of general laws.

9. To ascertain the bearing of the spark drawn from the electric machine under every variety of circumstances, that we thus may be emboldened with Franklin to address, in the form of a kite, the question to the cloud about the nature of the lightning. To assure ourselves of the manner in which bodies fall with the exactness of a Galileo, that with Newton we may dare to ask the Moon about the force that fastens it to the Earth.

10. In short, by the value we set upon truth, by our hope in a steady and universal progress, not to permit a tyrannical prejudice to neglect or mutilate unwelcome facts, but to rear the superstructure of science upon the broad and unchangeable basis of full attention paid to the most isolated as well as the most frequent phenomena.

"Rearing the superstructure of science..." simply put means : Science – careful observation and our obedience to natural laws – helps us move from belief to knowledge. We can believe whatever we like, but unless we arrive at knowledge (and ultimately truth), that belief is useless and can be discarded.

As an exercise, go ask yourself all the things you believe, and how many of them you actually know for sure and first hand. You will come to the conclusion that most of the information you have accepted as truth has come from others, which – coincidentally – was their thinking, not yours! You know by now what this means and how to protect yourself against it.

11. An ever-increasing material may be collected by observation, but the accumulated facts are of very different value for the explanation of nature, and as we esteem most highly those useful qualities of men which are of the rarest occurrence, so does natural philosophy sift the facts and attach a pre-eminent importance to that striking class which cannot be accounted for by the usual and daily observation of life.

12. If then, we find that certain persons seem to possess unusual power, what are we to conclude? First, we may say, it is not so, which is simply an acknowledgment of our lack of information because every honest investigator admits that there are many strange and previously unaccountable phenomena constantly taking place. Those, however, who become acquainted with the creative power of thought, will no longer consider them unaccountable.

13. Second, we may say that they are the result of supernatural interference, but a scientific understanding of Natural Laws will convince us that there is nothing supernatural. Every phenomenon is the result of an accurate definite cause, and the cause is an immutable law or principle, which operates with invariable precision, whether the law is put into operation consciously or unconsciously.

14. Third, we may say that we are on »forbidden ground,« that there are some things which we should not know. This objection was used against every advance in human knowledge. Every individual who ever advanced a new idea, whether a Columbus, a Darwin, a Galileo, a Fulton or an Emerson, was subjected to ridicule or persecution, so that this objection should receive no serious consideration, but, on the contrary, we should carefully consider every fact which is brought to our attention; by doing this we will more readily ascertain the law upon which it is based.

15. It will be found that **the creative power of thought will explain every possible condition or experience**, whether physical, mental or spiritual.

16. Thought will bring about conditions in correspondence with the predominant mental attitude. Therefore, if we fear disaster, as fear is a powerful form of thought, disaster will be

the certain result of our thinking. It is this form of thought which frequently sweeps away the result of many years of toil and effort.

17.　If we think of some form of material wealth we may secure it. By concentrated thought the required conditions will be brought about, and the proper effort put forth, which will result in bringing about the circumstances necessary to realize our desires; but we often find that when we secure the things we thought we wanted, they do not have the effect we expected. That is, the satisfaction is only temporary, or possibly is the reverse of what we expected.

18.　What, then, is the proper method of procedure? What are we to think in order to secure what we really desire? What you and I desire, what we all desire, what every one is seeking, is **Happiness and Harmony**. If we can be truly happy we shall have everything the world can give. If we are happy ourselves we can make others happy.

19.　But we cannot be happy unless we have, health, strength, congenial friends, pleasant environment, sufficient supply, not only to take care of our necessities **but to provide for those comforts and luxuries to which we are entitled**.

20.　The old orthodox way of thinking was to be »a worm,« to be satisfied with our portion whatever it is; but the modern idea is to know that we are entitled to the best of everything, that the »**Father and I are one**« and that **the »Father« is the Universal Mind**, the Creator, the Original Substance from which all things proceed.

21.　Now admitting that his is all true in theory, and it has been taught for two thousand years, and is the essence of every system of Philosophy or Religion, how are we to make it practical in our lives? How are we to get the actual, tangible results here and now?

What you and I desire, what we all desire,
what every one is seeking, is Happiness and Harmony.

Thought will create nothing unless it is consciously, systematically, and constructively directed.

22. In the first place, we must put our knowledge into practice. Nothing can be accomplished in any other way. The athlete may read books and lessons on physical training all his life, but unless he begins to give out strength by actual work he will never receive any strength; he will eventually get exactly what he gives; but he will have to give it first. It is exactly the same with us; we will get exactly what we give, but we shall have to give it first. It will then return to us manyfold, and the **giving is simply a mental process**, because thoughts are causes and conditions are effects; therefore in giving thoughts of courage, inspiration, health or help of any kind we are setting causes in motion which will bring about their effect.

23. Thought is a spiritual activity and is therefore creative, but make no mistake, thought will create nothing unless it is consciously, systematically, and constructively directed; and herein is the difference between idle thinking, which is simply a dissipation of effort, and constructive thinking, which means practically unlimited achievement.

24. We have found that everything we get comes to us by the Law of Attraction. **A happy thought cannot exist in an unhappy consciousness**; therefore the consciousness must change, and, as the consciousness changes, all conditions necessary to meet the changed consciousness must gradually change, in order to meet the requirements of the new situation.

25. In creating a Mental Image or an Ideal, we are projecting a thought into the Universal Substance from which all things are created. This Universal Substance is Omnipresent, Omnipotent and Omniscient. Are **we** to inform the Omniscient as to the proper channel to be used to materialize our demand? Can the **finite** advise the Infinite? This is the cause of failure; of every failure. We recognize the Omnipresence of

the Universal Substance, but we fail to appreciate the fact that this substance is not only Omnipresent, but is Omnipotent and Omniscient, and consequently will set causes in motion concerning which we may be entirely ignorant.

26. **We can best conserve our interests by recognizing the Infinite Power and Infinite Wisdom of the Universal Mind**, and in this way become a channel whereby the Infinite can bring about the realization of our desire. This means that recognition brings about realization, therefore for your exercise this week make use of the principle, recognize the fact that you are a part of the whole, and that a part must be the same in kind and quality as the whole; the only difference there can possibly be, is in degree.

27. When this tremendous fact begins to permeate your consciousness, when you really come into a realization of the fact that you (not your body, but the Ego), the »I,« the spirit which thinks, is an integral part of the great whole; that it is the same in substance, in quality, in kind; that the Creator could create nothing different from Himself, you will also be able to say, »**The Father and I are one**« and you will come into an understanding of the beauty, the grandeur, the transcendental opportunities which have been placed at your disposal.

"A man might frame and let loose a star,
to roll in its orbit, and yet not have done
so memorable a thing before God as he
who lets a golden-orbed thought to roll
through the generations of time."
— H. W. BEECHER

PART THIRTEEN — QUESTIONS AND ANSWERS

121. *What is the method by which natural philosophers obtain and apply their knowledge?*
To observe individual facts carefully, patiently, accurately, with all the instruments and resources at their command, before venturing upon a statement of general laws.

122. *How may we be certain that this method is correct?*
By not permitting a tyrannical prejudice to neglect or mutilate unwelcome facts.

123. *What class of facts are esteemed most highly?*
Those which cannot be accounted for by the usual daily observation of life.

124. *Upon what is this principle founded?*
Upon reason and experience.

125. *What does it destroy?*
Superstition, precedent and conventionality.

126. *How have these laws been discovered?*
By a generalization of facts which are uncommon, rare, strange and form the exception.

127. *How may we account for much of the strange and heretofore unexplainable phenomena which is constantly taking place?*
By the creative power of thought.

128. *Why is this so?*
Because when we learn of a fact we can be sure that it is the result of a certain definite cause and that this cause will operate with invariable precision.

129. *What is the result of this knowledge?*
It will explain the cause of every possible condition, whether physical, mental or spiritual.

130. *How will our best interest be conserved?*
By a recognition of the fact that a knowledge of the creative nature of thought puts us in touch with infinite power.

This is the hard mental labour you have to provide, for nothing else would develop your consciousness any other way. It is no longer good enough, or to your benefit, to just believe what you are being told or presented with. Please refer back to Part 8, where you learn how to ascertain the cause, and change your thought in order to start a new chain of causation.

THE DISCIPLINE OF THINKING

You have found from your study thus far that thought is a spiritual activity and is therefore endowed with creative power. This does not mean that some thought is creative, but that all thought is creative. This same principle can be brought into operation in a negative way, through the process of denial.

The Conscious and Subconscious are but two phases of action in connection with one mind. The relation of the Subconscious to the Conscious is quite analogous to that existing between a weather vane and the atmosphere. Just as the least pressure of the atmosphere causes an action on the part of the weather vane, so does the least thought entertained by the Conscious Mind produce within your Subconscious Mind action in exact proportion to the depth of feeling characterizing the thought and the intensity with which the thought is indulged.

It follows that if you deny unsatisfactory conditions, you are withdrawing the creative power of your thought from these conditions. You are cutting them away at the root. You are sapping their vitality.

Remember that the Law of Growth necessarily governs every manifestation in the objective, so that **a denial of unsatisfactory conditions will not bring about instant change**. A plant will remain visible for some time after its roots have been cut, but it will gradually fade away and eventually disappear, so the withdrawal of your thought from the contemplation of unsatisfactory conditions will gradually, but surely, terminate these conditions.

You will see that this is an exactly opposite course from the one which we would naturally be inclined to adopt. It will therefore have an exactly opposite effect to the one usually secured. **Most persons concentrate intently upon unsatisfactory conditions, thereby giving the condition that measure of energy and vitality which is necessary in order to supply a vigorous growth**.

THE DISCIPLINE OF THINKING

I.   The Universal Energy in which all motion, light, heat, and colour have their origin, does not partake of the limitation

"Concentrating upon unsatisfactory conditions" is of course not really clever, albeit still understandable, as your reality is being constructed through your five senses. These reflect the result of past thinking (yours and/or that of others), for which you have subsequently developed corresponding synaptic connections ("wiring") in your brain.

of the many effects of which it is the cause, but it is supreme over them all. This Universal Substance is the source of all Power, Wisdom and Intelligence.

2. To recognize this Intelligence is to acquaint yourself with the knowing quality of mind, and through it to move upon the Universal Substance, and bring it into harmonious relations in your affairs.

3. This is something that the most learned physical science teacher has not attempted — a field of discovery upon which he has not yet launched. In fact, but few of the materialistic schools have ever caught the first ray of this light. It does not seem to have dawned upon them that **wisdom is just as much present everywhere as are force and substance**.

4. Some will say, if these principles are true, why are we not demonstrating them? As the fundamental principle is obviously correct, why do we not get proper results? We do. **We get results in exact accordance with our understanding of the law and our ability to make the proper application**. We secured no results from the laws governing electricity until someone formulated the law and showed us how to apply it.

5. This puts us in an entirely new relation to our environment, opening up possibilities previously undreamed of, and this by an orderly sequence of law which is naturally involved in our new mental attitude.

6. Mind is creative and the principle upon which this law is based is sound and legitimate and is inherent in the nature of things. This creative power does not originate in the individual, but in the Universal, which is the source and fountain of all energy and substance; **the individual is simply the channel for the distribution of this energy**. The individual is the means by which the Universal produces the various combinations which result in the formation of phenomena.

7. We know that scientists have resolved matter into an immense number of molecules; these molecules have been resolved into atoms, and the atoms into electrons. The discovery of electrons in high vacuum glass tubes containing fused terminals of hard metal, indicates conclusively that these

electrons fill all space; that they exist everywhere, that they are omnipresent. They fill all material bodies and occupy the whole of what we call empty space. This, then, is the Universal Substance from which all things proceed.

8. Electrons would forever remain electrons unless directed where to go to be assembled into atoms and molecules, and this director is mind. A number of electrons revolving around a centre of force constitutes an atom; atoms unite in absolutely regular mathematical ratios and form molecules, and these unite with each other to form a multitude of compounds which unite to build the Universe.

9. The lightest known atom is hydrogen and this is 1,700 times heavier than an electron. An atom of mercury is 300,000 times heavier than an electron. Electrons are pure negative electricity, and as they have the same potential velocity as all other cosmic energy, such as heat, light, electricity and thought (186,282 miles per second), neither time nor space require consideration.

10. The manner in which the velocity of light was ascertained is interesting. The velocity of light was obtained by the Danish astronomer **Ole Rømer** in 1676, by observing the eclipses of Jupiter's moons. When the Earth was nearest to Jupiter, the eclipse appeared about eight and one-half minutes too soon for the calculations, and when the Earth was most remote from Jupiter, they were about eight and one-half minutes too late. Rømer concluded the reason to be that it required 17 minutes for light from the planet to traverse the diameter of the Earth's orbit, which measured the difference of the distances of the Earth from Jupiter. This calculation has since been verified, and proves that light travels about 186,000 miles a second.

Ole Christensen Rømer
(1644 – 1710)

11. Electrons manifest in the body as cells, and **possess mind and intelligence sufficient for them to perform their functions in the human physical anatomy**. Every part of the body is composed of cells, some of which operate independently; others in communities. Some are busy building tissue, while others are engaged in forming the various secretions necessary for the body. Some act as carriers of

material; others are the surgeons whose work it is to repair damage; others are scavengers, carrying off waste; others are constantly ready to repel invaders or other undesirable intruders of the germ family.

12. All these cells are moving for a common purpose and each one is not only a living organism, but has sufficient intelligence to enable it to perform its necessary duties. It is also endowed with sufficient intelligence to conserve the energies and perpetuate its own life. It must, therefore, secure sufficient nourishment and it has been found that it exercises choice in the selection of such nourishment.

13. Each cell is born, reproduces itself, dies and is absorbed. The maintenance of health and life itself depends upon the constant regeneration of these cells.

14. It is therefore apparent that there is mind in every atom of the body. This mind is negative mind, and **the power of the individual to think makes him positive, so that he can control this negative mind**. This is the scientific explanation for metaphysical healing, and will enable anyone to understand the principle upon which this remarkable phenomenon rests.

15. This negative mind, which is contained in every cell of the body, has been called the Subconscious Mind, because it acts without our conscious knowledge. We have found that this Subconscious Mind is responsive to the will of the Conscious Mind.

Remember: negative isn't about being "bad", but about being indifferent as to the input received. And as you can see, this attribute fits exactly onto the Subconscious Mind, which simply follows orders and converts them into what we then perceive as our reality.

16. All things have their origin in mind, and appearances are the result of thought, so that we see that **things in themselves have no origin, permanency, or reality**. Since they are produced by thought, they can be erased by thought.

17. In mental, as in natural science, experiments are being made and each discovery lifts man one step higher toward his possible goal. We find that every man is the reflection of the thought he has entertained during his lifetime. This is stamped on his face, his form, his character, his environment.

Much more on this you will find in Charles Haanel's book, "*A Book about YOU*".

18. Back of every effect there is a cause, and if we follow the trail to its starting point, we shall find the creative principle out

169

of which it grew. Proofs of this are now so complete that this truth is generally accepted.

19. The objective world is controlled by an unseen and, heretofore, unexplainable power. We have, heretofore, personalized this power and called it God. We have now, however, learned to look upon it as the **permeating essence or Principle** of all that exists — the Infinite or Universal Mind.

20. The Universal Mind, being infinite and omnipotent, has unlimited resources at its command, and when we remember that it is also omnipresent, we cannot escape the conclusion that we must be an expression or manifestation of that mind.

21. A recognition and understanding of the resources of the Subconscious Mind will indicate that the only difference between the Subconscious and the Universal is one of degree. They differ only as a drop of water differs from the ocean. They are the same in kind and quality, the difference is one of degree only.

22. Do you, can you, appreciate the value of this all-important fact; do you realize that a recognition of this tremendous fact places you **in touch with Omnipotence**? The Subconscious Mind being the connecting link between the Universal Mind and the Conscious Mind, is it not evident that the Conscious Mind can consciously suggest thoughts which the Subconscious Mind will put into action, and as the Subconscious is one with the Universal, is it not evident that no limit can be placed upon its activities?

23. A scientific understanding of this principle will explain the wonderful results which are secured through **the power of prayer**. The results which are secured in this way are not brought about by any special dispensations of providence, but on the contrary, they are the result of **the operation of a perfectly natural law**. There is, therefore, nothing either religious or mysterious about it.

24. Yet there are many who are not ready to enter into the discipline necessary to think correctly, even though it is evident that wrong thinking has brought failure.

25. **Thought is the only reality**; conditions are but the outward manifestations. As the thought changes, all outward or mate-

Gregg Braden has written about this in his book "*The Lost Mode of Prayer*".

Your prayer should therefore always be one of gratitude, and never one of request or desire.

170

rial conditions **must change** in order to be in harmony with their creator, which is thought.

26. But the thought must be clear cut, steady, fixed, definite, unchangeable. You cannot take one step forward and two steps backward, neither can you spend twenty or thirty years of your life building up negative conditions as the result of negative thoughts, and then expect to see them all melt away as the result of fifteen or twenty minutes of right thinking.

27. If you enter into the discipline necessary to bring about a radical change in your life, you must do so **deliberately**, after giving the matter **careful thought and full consideration**, and then you must allow **nothing** to interfere with your decision.

28. This discipline, this change of thought, this mental attitude will not only bring you the material things which are necessary for your highest and best welfare, but will bring health and harmonious conditions generally.

29. If you wish harmonious conditions in your life, you must develop an **harmonious mental attitude**.

30. Your world without will be a reflection of your world within.

31. For your exercise this week, concentrate on Harmony, and when I say concentrate, I mean all that the word implies; concentrate so deeply, so earnestly, **that you will be conscious of nothing but harmony**. Remember, we learn by doing. Reading these lessons will get you nowhere. It is in the practical application that the value consists.

If you deny unsatisfactory conditions, you are withdrawing the creative power of your thought from these conditions.

131. *What is the source of all Wisdom, Power and Intelligence?*
The Universal Mind.

132. *Where do all motion, light, heat and color have their origin?*
In the Universal Energy, which is one
manifestation of the Universal Mind.

133. *Where does the creative power of thought originate?*
In the Universal Mind.

134. *What is thought?*
Mind in motion.

135. *How is the Universal differentiated in form?*
The individual is the means by which the
Universal produces the various combinations
which result in formation of phenomena.

136. *How is this accomplished?*
The power of the individual to think is his ability to act
upon the Universal and bring it into manifestation.

137. *What is the first form which the Universal
takes so far as we know?*
Electrons, which fill all space.

138. *Where do all things have their origin?*
In mind.

139. *What is the result of a change of thought?*
A change in conditions.

140. *What is the result of a harmonious mental attitude?*
Harmonious conditions in life. Thought, immaterial though
it may be, is the matrix that shapes the issues of life.

*"Learn to keep the door shut, keep out
of your mind and out of your world,
every element that seeks admittance
with no definite helpful end in view."*
— GEORGE MATTHEW ADAMS

15

CONSCIOUS COOPERATION WITH NATURAL LAWS

Experiments with parasites found on plants indicate that even the lowest order of life is enabled to take advantage of natural law. This experiment was made by Jacques Loeb, M.D., Ph. D., a member of the Rockefeller Institute.

»In order to obtain the material, potted rose bushes are brought into a room and placed in front of a closed window. If the plants are allowed to dry out, the aphids (parasites), previously wingless, change to winged insects. After the metamorphosis, the animals leave the plants, fly to the window and then creep upward on the glass.«

It is evident that these tiny insects found that the plants on which they had been thriving were dead, and that they could therefore secure nothing more to eat and drink from this source. The only method by which they could save themselves from starvation was to grow temporary wings and fly, which they did.

Experiments such as these indicate that Omniscience as well as Omnipotence is omnipresent and that the tiniest living thing can take advantage of it in an emergency.

Part Fifteen will tell you more about the law under which we live. It will explain that **these laws operate to our advantage**; that **all conditions and experiences that come to us are for our benefit**; that we gain strength in proportion to the effort expended, and that our happiness is best attained through a conscious cooperation with natural laws.

CONSCIOUS COOPERATION WITH NATURAL LAWS

1. The laws under which we live are designed solely for our advantage. These laws are immutable and we cannot escape from their operation.
2. All the great eternal forces act in solemn silence, but it is in our power **to place ourselves in harmony with them** and thus express a life of comparative peace and happiness.
3. Difficulties, disharmonies, and obstacles, indicate that we are either **refusing to give up** what we no longer need, or **refusing to accept** what we require.

You are of course perfectly entitled to view both conditions and experiences as something bad or negative, as bad luck or fate or destiny. Whichever may be the case, they will continue to hang around your life with the obvious consequences. Thought is creative, irrespective of its direction. You aren't, however, creating for the sake of it, but for creating something beautiful and lasting.

Fifteen weeks into the course, you will find it increasingly easy to let go of that which you don't require, and accept with open arms that which you would like to see manifested in your life. Old habits may die hard, but you by now you know how to eradicate them. If not, I would like to refer you back to Part 14, but also earlier parts, which tell you exactly how this is being accomplished.

4. Growth is attained through an exchange of the old for the new, of the good for the better; it is a conditional or reciprocal action, for each of us is a complete thought entity and this completeness makes it possible for us to receive only as we give.

5. We cannot obtain what we lack if we tenaciously cling to what we have. We are able to consciously control our conditions as we come to sense the purpose of what we attract, and are able to extract from each experience only what we require for our further growth. Our ability to do this determines the degree of harmony or happiness we attain.

6. The ability to appropriate what we require for our growth, continually increases as we reach higher planes and broader visions, and the greater our abilities to know what we require, the more certain we shall be to discern its presence, to attract it and to absorb it. Nothing may reach us except what is necessary for our growth.

7. All conditions and experiences that come to us do so for our benefit. **Difficulties and obstacles will continue to come until we absorb their wisdom and gather from them the essentials of further growth.**

8. That we reap what we sow is mathematically exact. We gain permanent strength exactly to the extent of the effort required to overcome difficulties.

9. The inexorable requirements of growth demand that we exert the greatest degree of attraction for what is perfectly in accord with us. Our highest happiness will be best attained through our understanding of, and conscious cooperation with natural laws.

10. **In order to possess vitality, thought must be impregnated with love**. Love is a product of the emotions. It is therefore essential that the emotions be controlled and guided by the intellect and reason.

11. It is love which imparts vitality to thought and thus enables it to germinate. The Law of Attraction, or the Law of Love, for they are one and the same, will bring to it the necessary material for its growth and maturity.

Our highest happiness will be best attained through our understanding of, and conscious cooperation with natural laws.

12. The first form which thought will find is language, or words; this determines the **importance of words**; they are the first manifestation of thought — the vessels in which thought is carried. They take hold of the ether and by setting it in motion reproduce the thought to others in the form of sound.

13. Thought may lead to action of any kind, but whatever the action, it is simply the thought attempting to express itself in visible form. It is evident, therefore, that if we wish desirable conditions, we can afford to entertain only desirable thoughts.

14. This leads to the inevitable conclusion that if we wish to express abundance in our lives, we can afford to think abundance only, and as words are only thoughts taking form, **we must be especially careful to use nothing but constructive and harmonious language**, which when finally crystallized into objective forms, will prove to our advantage.

15. We cannot escape from the pictures we incessantly photograph on the mind, and this photography of erroneous conceptions is exactly what is being done by the use of words, when we use any form of language which is not identified with our welfare.

16. **We manifest more and more life as our thought becomes clarified and takes higher planes**. This is obtained with greater facility as we use words that are clearly defined, and relieved of the conceptions attached to them on lower planes of thought.

17. It is with words that we must express our thoughts, and if we are to make use of higher forms of truth, we may use only such material as has been carefully and intelligently selected with this purpose in view.

18. This wonderful power of clothing thoughts in the form of words is what differentiates Man from the rest of the animal kingdom; by the use of the written word he has been enabled

Here is another great exercise. Carefully observe yourself while speaking. "Watch your mouth!", is what we were told as children, when we used foul language. Over time, you will find yourself using words far more carefully and selectively. The mere fact that you have observed this yourself will give you great satisfaction. As with everything, it's constant practice that makes perfect.

176

to look back over the centuries and see the stirring scenes by which he has come into his present inheritance.

19. He has been enabled to come into communion with the greatest writers and thinkers of all time, and the combined record which we possess today is therefore the expression of Universal Thought as it has been seeking to take form in the mind of Man.

20. We know that the Universal Thought has for its goal the creation of form, and we know that the individual thought is likewise forever attempting to express itself in form, and we know that the word is a thought form, and a sentence is a combination of thought forms. Therefore, if we wish our ideal to be beautiful or strong, we must see that the words out of which this temple will eventually be created are exact; that they are put together carefully, because accuracy in building words and sentences is the highest form of architecture in civilization and is a passport to success.

21. Words are thoughts and are therefore an invisible and invincible power which will finally objectify themselves in the form they are given.

22. Words may become mental places that will live forever, or they may become shacks which the first breeze will carry away. They may delight the eye as well as the ear; they may contain all knowledge; in them we find the history of the past as well as the hope of the future; they are living messengers from which every human and superhuman activity is born.

23. The beauty of the word consists in the beauty of the thought; the power of the word consists in the power of the thought, and the power of the thought consists in its **vitality**. How shall we identify a vital thought? What are its distinguishing

Accuracy in building words and sentences
is the highest form of architecture in civilization,
and is a passport to success.

characteristics? It must have **principle**. How shall we identify principle?

24. There is a principle of Mathematics, but none of error; there is a principle of health, but none of disease; there is a principle of truth, but none of dishonesty; there is a principle of light, but none of darkness, and there is a principle of abundance, but none of poverty.

25. How shall we know that this is true? Because if we apply the principle of Mathematics correctly, we shall be certain of our results. Where there is health there will be no disease. If we know the Truth we cannot be deceived by error. If we let in light there can be no darkness, and where there is abundance there can be no poverty.

26. These are self-evident facts, but the all-important truth that **a thought containing principle is vital and therefore contains life** and consequently takes root, and eventually but surely and certainly displaces the negative thoughts, which by their very nature can contain no vitality, is one which seems to have been overlooked.

27. But this is a fact which will enable you to destroy every manner of discord, lack and limitation.

28. There can be no question but that he who »is wise enough to understand« will readily recognize that the creative power of thought places an invincible weapon in his hands and makes him a master of destiny.

29. In the physical world there is a Law of Compensation which is that »the appearance of a given amount of energy anywhere means the disappearance of the same amount somewhere else,« and so we find that we can get only what we give; if we pledge ourselves to a certain action we must be prepared to assume the responsibility for the development of that action. The Subconscious cannot reason. It takes us at our word; we have asked for something; we are now to receive it; we have made our bed, we are now to lie in it; the die has been cast; the threads will carry out the pattern we have made.

30. For this reason Insight must be exercised so that the thought which we entertain contains no mental, moral or physical germ which we do not wish objectified in our lives.

This is very important to understand. Whatever we have called "bad" needs the "good" in order to have something to fight or destroy. It cannot exist out of itself as it lacks a vital principle.

Once understood, you will only express things that are true, for they have principle and thus vitality and therefore the capability of giving you "more", which is exactly what you are after. More for you, and more of the same for others, too!

"Wise enough to understand" is another Bible reference, namely Jeremia 9:12. Quote: "What man is wise enough to understand this? [...] Why has the land been ruined and laid waste like a desert that no one can cross? [God] said, "It is because they have forsaken my law, which I set before them; they have not obeyed me or followed my law."

If we took away the human aspect of God, what we are left with is exactly what Charles Haanel said in points 24 and 25. "...*forsaken my law*" means exactly that. They didn't understand that everything is subject to Universal Law, and they didn't know that they had to bring themselves into alignment with the Universal Mind, expressing this accordingly through their harmonious and thus beautiful thoughts, words and actions. Consequently they did things that resulted in death and destruction. No divine providence, just cause and effect.

178

31. Insight is a faculty of the mind whereby we are enabled to examine facts and conditions at long range, a kind of human telescope; it enables us to understand the difficulties, as well as the possibilities, in any undertaking.

32. Insight enables us to be prepared for the obstacles which we shall meet; we can therefore overcome them before they have any opportunity of causing difficulty.

33. Insight enables us to plan to advantage and turn our thought and attention in the right direction, instead of into channels which can yield no possible return.

34. **Insight** is therefore absolutely essential for the development of any great achievement, and with it we may enter, explore and possess any mental field.

35. Insight is a product of the world within and is developed in the Silence, by concentration.

36. For your exercise this week, concentrate on Insight; take your accustomed position and focus the thought on the fact that to have a knowledge of the creative power of thought does not mean to possess the art of thinking. Let the thought dwell on the fact that knowledge does not apply itself. That our actions are not governed by knowledge, but by custom, precedent and habit. That the only way we can get ourselves to apply knowledge is by **a determined conscious effort**. Call to mind the fact that knowledge unused passes from the mind, that the value of the information is in the application of the principle; continue this line of thought until you gain sufficient insight to formulate a definite program for applying this principle to your own particular problem.

141. *What determines the degree of harmony which we attain?*
Our ability to appropriate what we require
for our growth from each experience.

142. *What do difficulties and obstacles indicate?*
That they are necessary for our wisdom and
spiritual growth.

143. *How may these difficulties be avoided?*
By a conscious understanding of and
cooperation with natural laws.

144. *What is the principle by which thought manifests itself
in form?*
The Law of Attraction.

145. *How is the necessary material secured by which the growth,
development and maturity of the idea take form?*
The Law of Love, which is the creative principle of the
Universe, imparts vitality to the thought, and the Law of
Attraction brings the necessary substance by the
Law of Growth.

146. *How are desirable conditions secured?*
By entertaining desirable thoughts only.

147. *How are undesirable conditions brought about?*
By thinking, discussing and visualizing conditions
of lack, limitation, disease, disharmony and discord
of every kind. This mental photography of erroneous
conceptions is taken up by the Subconscious and the Law
of Attraction will inevitably crystallize it into objective
form. That we reap what we sow is scientifically exact.

148. *How can we overcome every kind of fear,
lack, limitation, poverty and discord?*
By substituting principle for error.

149. *How may we recognize principle?*
By a conscious realization of the fact that Truth invariably
destroys error. We do not have to laboriously shovel the
darkness out; all that is necessary is to turn on the light.
The same principle applies to every form of
negative thought.

150. *What is the value of Insight?*

It enables us to understand the value of making application of the knowledge which we gain. Many seem to think that knowledge will automatically apply itself, which is by no means true.

*"Think truly, and thy thoughts shall the
world's famine feed; Speak truly, and each
word of thine shall be a fruitful seed;
Live truly, and thy life shall be
A great and noble creed."*
— HORATIO BONAR

16

CREATING SCIENTIFICALLY TRUE IDEALS

PART SIXTEEN

In the Hermetic Tradition, "Periodicity" is also called "Rhythm". Rhythm balances; rhythm creates waves and therefore polarity, or contrasts; rhythm allows us to measure and therefore to perceive, thus live.

Rhythm also gives us certainty. It als helps us with doing the right thing at the right time. By its very nature it shows us that not everything is beneficial all the time. Rhythm teaches us when to be active, and when to be passive, observant and risk-averse.

The vibratory activities of the planetary Universe are governed by the **Law of Periodicity**. Everything that lives has periods of birth, growth, fruitage, and decline. These periods are governed by the Septimal Law.

The **Law of Sevens** governs the days of the week, the phases of the moon, the harmonies of sound, light, heat, electricity, magnetism, and atomic structure. It governs the life of individuals and of nations, and it dominates the activities of the commercial world.

Life is growth, and growth is change; each seven years period takes us into a new cycle. The first seven years is the period of **infancy**. The next seven the period of **childhood**, representing the beginning of individual responsibility. The next seven represents the period of **adolescence**. The fourth period marks the attainment of **full growth**. The fifth period is the **constructive period**, when men begin to acquire property, possessions, a home and family. The next from 35 to 42, is a period of **reactions and changes**, and this in turn is followed by a period of **reconstruction, adjustment and recuperation**, so as to be ready for a new cycle of sevens, beginning with the fiftieth year.

There are many who think that the world is just about to pass out of the sixth period; that it will soon enter into the seventh period, the period of readjustment, reconstruction and harmony; the period which is frequently referred to as the Millennium.

Those familiar with these cycles will not be disturbed when things seem to go wrong, but can apply the principle outlined in these lessons with the full assurance that **a higher law will invariably control all other laws**, and that through an understanding and conscious operation of spiritual laws, we can convert every seeming difficulty into a blessing.

CREATING SCIENTIFICALLY TRUE IDEALS

I.   Wealth is a product of labour. **Capital is an effect, not a cause**; a servant, not a master; a means, not an end.

2. The most commonly accepted definition of wealth is that it consists of all useful and agreeable things which possess **exchange value**. It is this exchange value which is the predominant characteristic of wealth.

3. When we consider the small addition made by wealth to the happiness of the possessor, we find that **the true value consists not in its utility but in its exchange**.

4. This exchange value makes it a medium for securing **the things of real value** whereby our ideals may be realized.

5. Wealth should then never be desired as an end, but simply as **a means of accomplishing an end**. Success is contingent upon a higher ideal than the mere accumulation of riches, and he who aspires to such success must formulate an ideal for which he is willing to strive.

6. With such an ideal in mind, the ways and means can and will be provided, but the mistake must not be made of substituting the means for the end. **There must be a definite fixed purpose, an ideal**.

7. **Prentice Mulford** said: »*The man of success is the man possessed of the greatest spiritual understanding and every great fortune comes of superior and truly spiritual power.*« Unfortunately, there are those who fail tto recognize this power; they forget that Andrew Carnegie's mother had to help support the family when they came to America, that Harriman's father was a poor clergyman with a salary of only $200.00 a year, that Sir Thomas Lipton started with only 25 cents. These men had no other power to depend upon, but it did not fail them.

8. The power to create depends entirely upon spiritual power; there are three steps: idealization, visualization and materialization. Every captain of industry depends upon this power exclusively. In an article in *Everybody's Magazine*, **Henry M. Flagler**, the Standard Oil multimillionaire, admitted that the secret of his success was his power to see a thing in its completeness. The following conversation with the reporter shows his power of idealization, concentration and visualization, all spiritual powers:

9. »Did you actually vision to yourself the whole thing? I mean, did you, or could you, really close your eyes and see the tracks?

Please refer back to Part 10, section 2: "All wealth is the offspring of power; possessions are of value only as they confer power."

Prentice Mulford (1834 – 1891)

Henry Morrison Flagler (1830 – 1913)

And the trains running? And hear the whistles blowing? Did you go as far as that?« »Yes.« »How clearly?« »Very clearly.«

10. Here we have a vision of the law, we see »cause and effect«, we see that thought necessarily precedes and determines action. If we are wise, we shall come into a realization of the tremendous fact that **no arbitrary condition can exist for a moment**, and that human experience is the result of an orderly and harmonious sequence.

11. The successful business man is more often than not an **idealist** and is every striving for higher and higher standards. The subtle forces of thought as they crystallize in our daily moods is what constitutes life.

12. Thought is the plastic material with which we build images of our growing conception of life. **Use determines its existence**. As in all other things our ability to recognize it and use it properly is the necessary condition for attainment.

13. Premature wealth is but the forerunner of humiliation and disaster, because we cannot permanently retain anything which we do not merit or which we have not earned.

14. The conditions with which we meet in the world without, correspond to the conditions which we find in the world within. This is brought about by the Law of Attraction. How then shall we determine what is to enter into the world within?

15. Whatever enters the mind through the senses or the Subjective Mind will impress the mind and result in a mental image which will become a pattern for the creative energies. These experiences are largely the result of environment, chance, past thinking and other forms of negative thought, and must be subjected to **careful analysis before being entertained**. On the other hand, we can form our own mental images, through our own interior processes of thought, regardless of the thoughts of others, regardless of exterior conditions, regardless of environment of every kind, and it is by the exercise of this power that we can control our own destiny, body, mind and soul.

16. It is by the exercise of this power that we take our fate out of the hands of chance, and consciously make for ourselves the

That's what we have our Conscious (or Subjective) Mind for! The Gatekeeper analyses before anything can enter into the mighty domain of the Subconscious, where no further questioning or argumentation takes place, only fulfilment; only execution.

186

experiences which we desire, because when we consciously realize a condition, that condition will eventually manifest in our lives. It is therefore evident that in the last analysis thinking is the one great cause in life.

17. Therefore, to control thought is to control circumstances, conditions, environment, and destiny.

18. How then are we to control thought; what is the process? To think is to create a thought, but the result of the thought will depend upon its form, its quality and its vitality.

19. The form will depend upon the mental images from which it emanates; this will depend upon **the depth of the impression**, the **predominance of the idea**, the **clarity of the vision**, the boldness of the image.

20. The quality depends upon its substance, and this depends upon the material of which the mind is composed; if this material has been woven from thoughts of vigour, strength, courage, and determination, the thought will possess these qualities.

21. And finally, the vitality depends upon the **feeling** with which the thought is impregnated. If the thought is constructive, it will possess vitality; it will have life; it will grow, develop, expand; it will be creative; it will attract to itself everything necessary for its complete development.

22. If the thought is destructive, it will have within itself the germ of its own dissolution; it will die, but in the process of dying, it will bring sickness, disease, and every other form of discord.

23. This we call evil, and when we bring it upon ourselves, some of us are disposed to attribute our difficulties to a Supreme Being, but this supreme being is simply mind in equilibrium.

24. It is neither good nor bad, it simply is.

25. Our ability to differentiate it into form is our ability to manifest good or evil.

26. Good and evil therefore are not entities, they are simply words which we use to indicate the result of our actions, and these actions are in turn predetermined by the character of our thought.

"Persons, places and things" have no place in the absolute, because they are all relative. They are effects, and they have no principle. They will all disappear with time; so what you have to create is something with principle, something of permanence.

It's a state of mind you're after, one of happiness and harmony. As they contain a vital principle, the Law of Correspondence will bring to you all that is required for their manifestation. For that you require Faith, "*the substance of the things unseen, the evidence of the things hoped for.*"

27. If our thought is constructive and harmonious we manifest good; if it is destructive and discordant we manifest evil.

28. If you desire to visualize a different environment, the process is simply **to hold the ideal in mind, until your vision has been made real**; give no thought to persons, places or things; these have no place in the absolute; the environment you desire will contain everything necessary; the right persons, and the right things will come at the right time and in the right place.

29. It is sometimes not plain how character, ability, attainment, achievement, environment and destiny can be controlled through the power of visualization, but this is an exact scientific fact.

30. You will readily see that what we think determines the quality of mind, and that the quality of mind in turn determines our ability and mental capacity, and you can readily understand that the improvement in our ability will naturally be followed by increase in attainment and a greater control of circumstances.

31. It will thus be seen that Natural laws work in a perfectly natural and harmonious manner; everything seems to »just happen.« If you want any evidence of this fact, simply compare results of your efforts in your own life, when your actions were prompted by high ideals and when you had selfish or ulterior motives in mind. You will need no further evidence.

32. If you wish to bring about the realization of any desire, form a mental picture of success in your mind, by consciously visualizing your desire; in this way you will be compelling success, you will be externalising it in your life by **scientific methods**.

33. We can only see what already exists in the objective world, but what we visualize, already exists in the spiritual world, and this visualization is a substantial token of what will one day appear in the objective world, **if we are faithful to our ideal**. The reason for this is not difficult; visualization is a form of imagination; this process of thinking forms impressions on the mind, and these impressions in turn form

concepts and ideals, and they in turn are the plans from which the Master Architect will weave the future.

34. The psychologists have come to the conclusion that there is but one sense, **the sense of feeling**, and that all other senses are but modifications of this one sense; this being true, we know why feeling is the very fountain head of power, why the emotions so easily overcome the intellect, and why we must put feeling into our thought, if we wish results. **Thought and feeling is the irresistible combination**.

35. Visualization must, of course, be directed by the will; we are to visualize exactly what we want; we must be careful not to let the imagination run riot. Imagination is a good servant but a poor master, and unless it is controlled it may easily lead us into all kinds of speculations and conclusions which have no basis or foundation of fact whatsoever. Every kind of plausible opinion is liable to be accepted without any analytical examination and the inevitable result is mental chaos.

36. We must therefore construct only such mental images as are known to be scientifically true. Subject every idea to a searching analysis and **accept nothing which is not scientifically exact**. When you do this you will attempt nothing but what you know you can carry out and success will crown your efforts; this is what businessmen call farsightedness; it is much the same as insight, and is one of the great secrets of success in all important undertakings.

"Scientifically true" refers to that which has principle, as well as your conscious capability to comprehend and express. Remember that you cannot express powers that you do not possess, but as these are subject to your will, they are subject to change.

37. For your exercise this week, try to bring yourself to a realization of the important fact that harmony and happiness are states of consciousness and do not depend upon the possession of things. That things are effects and come as a consequence of correct mental states, so that if we desire material possession of any kind our chief concern should be to acquire the mental attitude which will bring about the result desired.

Through an understanding and conscious operation of spiritual laws, we can convert every seeming difficulty into a blessing.

189

This mental attitude is brought about by a realization of our spiritual nature and our unity with the Universal Mind which is the substance of all things. This realization will bring about everything which is necessary for our complete enjoyment. This is scientific or correct thinking. When we succeed in bringing about this mental attitude, it is comparatively easy to **realize our desire as an already accomplished fact**. When we can do this we shall have found the »Truth« which makes us »free« from every lack or limitation of any kind.

151. *Upon what does wealth depend?*
      Upon an understanding of the creative nature of thought.

152. *Upon what does its true value consist?*
      Upon its exchange value.

153. *Upon what does success depend?*
      Upon spiritual power.

154. *Upon what does this power depend?*
      Upon use; use determines its existence.

155. *How may we take our fate out of the hands of chance?*
      By consciously realizing the conditions which
      we desire to see manifested in our lives.

156. *What then is the great business of life?*
      Thinking.

157. *Why is this so?*
      Because thought is spiritual and therefore creative.
      To consciously control thought is therefore to control
      circumstances, conditions, environment and destiny.

158. *What is the source of all evil?*
      Destructive thinking.

159. *What is the source of all good?*
      Scientific correct thinking.

160. *What is scientific thinking?*
      A recognition of the creative nature of spiritual
      energy and our ability to control it.

*"The greatest events of an age are
its best thoughts. It is the nature of
thought to find its way into action."*
— CHRISTIAN NESTELL BOVEE

INTUITIVE PERCEPTION THROUGH CONCENTRATION

PART SEVENTEEN

The kind of Deity which a man, consciously or unconsciously, worships, indicates the intellectual status of the worshipper.

Ask the Indian of God, and he will describe to you a powerful chieftain of a glorious tribe. Ask the Pagan of God, and he will tell you of a God of fire, a God of water, a god of this, that, and the other.

Ask the Israelite of God, and he will tell you of the God of Moses, who conceived it expedient to rule by coercive measures; hence, the Ten Commandments. Or of Joshua, who led the Israelites into battle, confiscated property, murdered the prisoners, and laid waste to cities.

The so-called heathen made »graven images« of their Gods, whom they were accustomed to worship, but among the most intelligent, at least, these images were but the visible fulcrums with which they were enabled to mentally concentrate on the qualities which they desired to externalise in their lives.

We of the twentieth century worship a God of Love in theory, but in practice we make for ourselves »graven images« of »Wealth,« »Power,« »Fashion,« »Custom« and »Conventionality.« We »fall down« before them and worship them. We concentrate on them and they are thereby externalised in our lives.

The student who masters the contents of Part Seventeen **will not mistake the symbols for the reality**; he will be interested in causes, rather than effects. He will concentrate on the realities of life, and will then not be disappointed in the results.

INTUITIVE PERCEPTION THROUGH CONCENTRATION

1. We are told that Man has »**dominion over all things**«; this dominion is established through mind. Thought is the activity which controls every principle beneath it. The highest principle by reason of its superior essence and qualities necessarily determines the circumstances, aspects and relation of everything with which it comes in contact.

2. The vibrations of mental forces are the finest and consequently the most powerful in existence. To those who perceive

Although Charles Haanel wrote "twentieth century", it is obvious that the same applies to the beginning of the twenty-first century, too.

A reference to the Bible, Psalm 8:6.

194

Spiritual insight requires a quickening of the vibrations of the Mind, and is only secured when the Mind is continuously concentrated in a given direction.

the nature and transcendency of mental force, all physical power sinks into insignificance.

3. We are accustomed to look upon the Universe with a lens of five senses, and from these experiences our anthropomorphic conceptions originate, but **true conceptions are only secured by spiritual insight**. This insight requires a quickening of the vibrations of the mind, and is only secured when the mind is continuously concentrated in a given direction.

4. **Continuous concentration means an even, unbroken flow of thought and is the result of a patient, persistent, persevering and well-regulated system**.

5. Great discoveries are the result of long-continued investigation. The science of mathematics requires years of concentrated effort to master it, and the greatest science — that of the mind — is revealed only through concentrated effort.

6. Concentration is much misunderstood; there seems to be an idea of effort or activity associated with it, when just the contrary is necessary. The greatness of an actor lies in the fact that he forgets himself in the portrayal of his character, becoming so identified with it, that the audience is swayed by the realism of the performance. This will give you a good idea of true concentration; you should be so interested in your thought, so engrossed in your subject, as to be conscious of nothing else. Such concentration leads to **intuitive perception and immediate insight** into the nature of the object concentrated upon.

7. All knowledge is the result of concentration of this kind; it is thus that the secrets of Heaven and Earth have been wrested;

it is thus that the mind becomes a magnet and the desire to know draws the knowledge, irresistibly attracts it, makes it your own.

8. Desire is largely subconscious; **conscious desire rarely realizes its object when the latter is out of immediate reach**. Subconscious desire arouses the latent faculties of the mind, and difficult problems seem to solve themselves.

9. The Subconscious Mind may be aroused and brought into action in any direction and made to serve us for any purpose, by concentration. The practice of concentration requires the control of the physical, mental, and spiritual being; **all modes of consciousness whether physical, mental, or spiritual, must be under control**.

10. Spiritual Truth is therefore the controlling factor; it is this which will enable you to grow out of limited attainment and reach a point where you will be able to translate modes of thought into character and consciousness.

11. Concentration does not mean mere thinking of thoughts, but the transmutation of these thoughts into practical values; the average person has no conception of the meaning of concentration. There is always the cry »to have« but never the cry »to be«; they fail to understand that they cannot have one without the other, that they must first find the »kingdom« before they can have the »things added.« Momentary enthusiasm is of no value; it is only with unbounded self-confidence that the goal is reached.

12. The mind may place the ideal a little too high and fall short of the mark; it may attempt to soar on untrained wings and instead of flying, fall to Earth; but that is no reason for not making another attempt.

13. Weakness is the only barrier to mental attainment; attribute your weakness to physical limitations or mental uncertainties

Concentration does not mean mere thinking of thoughts, but the transmutation of these thoughts into practical values.

All mental discovery and attainment
are the result of desire plus concentration.

and try again; **ease and perfection are gained by repetition**.

14. The astronomer centres his mind on the stars and they give forth their secrets; the geologists centres his mind on the construction of the Earth and we have geology; so with all things. Men centre their minds on the problems of life, and the result is apparent in the vast and complex social order of the day.

15. All mental discovery and attainment are the result of desire plus concentration; desire is the strongest mode of action; the more persistent the desire, the more authoritative the revelation. Desire added to concentration will wrench any secret from nature.

16. In realizing great thoughts, in experiencing great emotions that correspond with great thoughts, the mind is in a state where it **appreciates the value of higher things**.

17. The intensity of one moment's earnest concentration and the intense longing to become and to attain may take you further than years of slow normal and forced effort; it will unfasten the prison bars of unbelief, weakness, impotence and self-belittlement, and you will come into a realization of the joy of overcoming.

18. The spirit of initiative and originality is developed through persistence and continuity of mental effort. Business teaches the value of concentration and encourages decision of character; it develops practical insight and quickness of conclusion. The mental element in every commercial pursuit is dominant as the controlling factor, and desire is the predominating force; all commercial relations are the externalisation of desire.

19. Many of the sturdy and substantial virtues are developed in commercial employment; the mind is steadied and directed;

it becomes efficient. The principal necessity is the **strengthening of the mind** so that it rises superior to the distractions and wayward impulses of instinctive life and thus successfully overcomes in the conflict between the higher and lower self.

20. All of us are dynamos, but the dynamo of itself is nothing. The mind must work the dynamo; then it is useful and its energy can be definitely concentrated. The mind is an engine whose power is undreamed. Thought is an omni-working power. It is the ruler and creator of all form and all events occurring in form. Physical energy is nothing in comparison with the omnipotence of thought, because **thought enables man to harness all other natural power**.

21. Vibration is the action of thought; it is vibration which reaches out and attracts the material necessary to construct and build. There is nothing mysterious concerning the power of thought. Concentration simply implies that consciousness can be focussed to the point where it becomes identified with the object of its attention. As food absorbed is the essence of the body, so the mind absorbs the object of its attention, gives it life and being.

22. If you concentrate on some matter of importance, the intuitive power will be set in operation, and help will come in the nature of information which will lead to success.

23. Intuition arrives at conclusions without the aid of experience or memory. Intuition often solves problems that are beyond the grasp of the reasoning power. Intuition often comes with a suddenness that is startling; it reveals the truth for which we are searching, so directly that it seems to come from a higher power. **Intuition can be cultivated and developed**; in order to do this it must be **recognized** and **appreciated**. If the intuitive visitor is given a royal welcome when he comes, he will come again; the more cordial the welcome the more frequent his visits will become, but if he is ignored or neglected he will make his visits few and far apart.

24. **Intuition usually comes in the Silence**; great minds seek solitude frequently; it is here that all the larger problems of life are worked out. For this reason every businessman

Remember that fundamentally the Subconscious is omnipotent; there is no limit to the things that can be done when it is given the power to act.

who can afford it has a private office, where he will not be disturbed. If you cannot afford a private office, you can at least find somewhere, where you can be alone a few minutes each day, to train the thought along lines which will enable you to develop that invincible power which is necessary to achieve.

25. Remember that fundamentally the Subconscious is omnipotent; there is no limit to the things that can be done when it is given the power to act. Your degree of success is determined by the nature of your desire. If the nature of your desire is in harmony with Natural Law or the Universal Mind, it will gradually emancipate the mind and give you invincible courage.

26. Every obstacle conquered, every victory gained, will give you more faith in your power, and you will have greater ability to win. Your strength is determined by your mental attitude. If this attitude is one of success, and is permanently held with an unswerving purpose, you will attract to you from the invisible domain the things you **silently demand**.

27. By keeping the thought in mind, it will gradually take tangible form. A definite purpose sets causes in motion which go out in the invisible world and find the material necessary to serve your purpose.

28. You may be pursuing the symbols of power, instead of power itself. You may be pursuing fame instead of **honour**, riches instead of **wealth**, position instead of **servitude**; in either event you will find that they turn to ashes just as you overtake them.

29. Premature wealth or position cannot be retained because it has not been earned; we get only what we give, and

"Silently demand", because you assert your right to live an abundant life, and because you know both the underlying system and the mechanism for manifestation. It has become so ingrained in your system, that you take it for granted while continued use will bring your more of it time and time again.

199

those who try to get without giving always find that the law of compensation is relentlessly bringing about an exact equilibrium.

30. The race has usually been for money and other mere symbols of power, but **with an understanding of the true source of power, we can afford to ignore the symbols**. The man with a large bank account finds it unnecessary to load his pockets down with gold; so with the man who has found the true source of power; he is no longer interested in its shams or pretensions.

31. Thought ordinarily leads outwardly in evolutionary directions, but it can be turned within where it will take hold of the basic principles of things, the heart of things, the spirit of things. When you get to the heart of things it is comparatively easy to understand and command them.

32. This is because **the Spirit of a thing is the thing itself**, the vital part of it, the real substance. The form is simply the outward manifestation of the spiritual activity within.

33. For your exercise this week concentrate as nearly as possible in accordance with the method outlined in this lesson; let there be no conscious effort or activity associated with your purpose. Relax completely; avoid any thought of anxiety as to results. Remember that power comes through repose. Let the thought dwell upon your object **until it is completely identified with it**, until you are conscious of nothing else.

34. If you wish to eliminate fear, concentrate on **courage**.

35. If you wish to eliminate lack, concentrate on **abundance**.

36. If you wish to eliminate disease, concentrate on **health**.

37. **Always concentrate on the ideal as an already existing fact**; this is the germ cell, the life principle which goes forth and sets in motion those causes which guide, direct and bring about the necessary relation, which eventually manifest in form.

"To every man there openeth a way,
And the high soul climbs the high way,
And the low soul gropes the low;
And in between on the misty flats,
The rest drift to and fro.
But to every man there openeth
A high way and a low,
And every man decideth
The way his soul shall go."
— JOHN OXENHAM

161. *What is the true method of concentration?*
To become so identified wit the object of your
thought that you are conscious of nothing else.

162. *What is the result of this method of concentration?*
Invisible forces are set in motion which irresistibly bring
about conditions in correspondence with your thought.

163. *What is the controlling factor in this method of thought?*
Spiritual Truth.

164. *Why is this so?*
Because the nature of our desire must
be in harmony with Natural Law.

165. *What is the practical value of this method of concentration?*
Thought is transmuted into character, and character is the
magnet which creates the environment of the individual.

166. *What is the controlling factor in every commercial pursuit?*
The mental element.

167. *Why is this so?*
Because mind is the ruler and creator of all
form and all events occurring in form.

168. *How does concentration operate?*
By the development of the powers of perception,
wisdom, intuition, and sagacity.

169. *Why is intuition superior to reason?*
Because it does not depend upon experience or memory
and frequently brings about the solution to our problems
by methods concerning which we are in entire ignorance.

170. *What is the result of pursuing the symbol of the reality?*
They frequently turn to ashes just as we overtake
them, because the symbol is only the outward form of
the spiritual activity within, therefore unless we can
possess the spiritual reality, the form disappears.

18
THE LAW OF ATTRACTION

In order to grow **we must obtain what is necessary for our growth**. This is brought about through the Law of Attraction. This principle is the sole means by which the individual is differentiated from the Universal.

Think for a moment, what would a man be if he were not a husband, father, or brother, if he were not interested in the social, economical, political or religious world. He would be nothing but an abstract theoretical ego. He exists, therefore, only in his **relation to the whole**, in his relation to other men, in his relation to society. This relation constitutes his environment and in no other way.

It is evident, therefore, that the individual is simply the differentiation of the one Universal Mind »which lighteth every man that cometh into the world,« and his so-called individuality or personality consists of nothing but the manner in which he relates with the whole.

This we call his environment and is brought about by the Law of Attraction. Part Eighteen, which follows, has something more to say concerning this important law.

THE LAW OF ATTRACTION

1. There is a change in the thought of the world. This change is silently transpiring in our midst, and is more important than any which the world has undergone since the downfall of Paganism.
2. These present revolution in the opinions of all classes of men, the highest and most cultured of men as well as those of the labouring class, stands unparalleled in the history of the world.
3. Science has of late made such vast discoveries, has revealed such an infinity of resources, has unveiled such enormous

Taken from the Bible, John 1:9. Interesting in this context also John 1:1 – "In the beginning was the Word, and the Word was with God, and the Word was God." An old German translation finished off with "...and God was the Word." As we know now, both are equally true, for the word is nothing but an effect of a corresponding thought, which is Mind in action – the Universal Mind in action; God in action! John 1:10 goes on saying: "He was in the world, and the world was made by him, and the world knew him not." In other words: we are of the Universal Mind, but the Universal Mind is not aware of it.

When you get to the heart of things it is comparatively easy to understand and command them.

204

possibilities and such unsuspected forces, that scientific men more and more hesitate to affirm certain theories as established and beyond doubt or to deny other theories as absurd or impossible.

4. A new civilization is being born; customs, creeds, and precedent are passing; **vision, faith and service are taking their place**. The fetters of tradition are being melted off from humanity, and as the impurities of materialism are being consumed, thought is being liberated and truth is rising fully robed before an astonished multitude.

5. The whole world is on the eve of a new consciousness, a new power, and a new realization within the self.

6. Physical science has resolved matter into molecules, molecules into atoms, atoms into energy, and it has remained for Mr. **J. A. Fleming**, in an address before the Royal Institution, to resolve this energy into mind. He says, »In its ultimate essence, energy may be incomprehensible by us except as an exhibition of **the direct operation of that which we call mind or will.**«

Sir John Ambrose Fleming
(1849 – 1945)

7. And this mind is the indwelling and ultimate. It is imminent in matter as in spirit. It is the sustaining, energizing, all pervading Spirit of the Universe.

8. Every living thing must be sustained by this omnipotent Intelligence, and we find the difference in individual lives to be largely measured by the degree of this intelligence, which they manifest. It is greater intelligence that places the animal in a higher scale of being than the plant, the man higher than the animal, and we find that this increased **intelligence is again indicated by the power of the individual to control modes of action and thus to consciously adjust himself to his environment**.

9. It is this adjustment that occupies the attention of the greatest minds, and this adjustment consists in nothing else than the recognition of an existing order in the Universal Mind, for **it is well known that this mind will obey us precisely in proportion as we first obey it**.

10. It is the recognition of Natural Laws that has enabled us to annihilate time and space, to soar in the air and to make iron

float, and the greater the degree of intelligence the greater will be our recognition of these Natural Laws and the greater will be the power we can possess.

11. It is the recognition of the self as an individualization of this Universal Intelligence that enables the individual to control those forms of intelligence which have not yet reached this level of self-recognition; they do not know that this Universal Intelligence permeates all things, ready to be called into action; they do not know that it is responsive to every demand, and they are therefore in bondage to the law of their own being.

12. Thought is creative and the principle on which the law is based is sound and legitimate and is inherent in the nature of things; but **this creative power does not originate in the individual, but in the Universal**, which is the source and foundation of all energy and substance; the individual is simply the channel for the distribution of this energy.

13. The individual is simply the means by which the universal produces the various combinations which result in the formation of phenomena, which depends upon the **Law of Vibration**, whereby various rates of rapidity of motion in the primary substance form new substances only in certain exact numerical ratios.

14. Thought is the invisible link by which the individual comes into communication with the Universal, the finite with the Infinite, the seen with the Unseen. Thought is the magic by which the human is transformed into a being who thinks and knows and feels and acts.

15. As the proper apparatus has enabled the eye to discover worlds without number millions of miles away, so, with the proper understanding, man has been enabled to communicate with the Universal Mind, the source of all power.

16. The understanding which is usually developed is about as valuable as a tape recorder without a tape; in fact, it is usually nothing more than a »belief«, which means nothing at all. The savages of the Cannibal Islands believe something, but that proves nothing.

The only belief which is of any value to anyone
is a belief that has been put to a test and demonstrated to be a fact;
that has become a living Faith or Truth.

17. The only belief which is of any value to anyone is a belief that has been put to a test and demonstrated to be a fact; it is then no longer a belief, but has become a living Faith or Truth.

18. And this Truth has been put to the test by hundreds of thousands of people and has been found to be the Truth exactly in proportion to the usefulness of the apparatus which they used.

19. A man would not expect to locate stars hundreds of millions of miles away without a sufficiently strong telescope, and for this reason Science is continually engaged in building larger and more powerful telescopes and is continually rewarded by additional knowledge of the heavenly bodies.

This is a lovely and very easy to understand analogy. The more powerful the tools, the deeper the insight and the resulting benefit, both on a physical and a mental level.

20. So with understanding; men are continually making progress in **the methods which they use to come into communication with the Universal Mind and its infinite possibilities**.

21. The Universal Mind manifests itself in the objective, through the principle of attraction that each atom has for every other atom, in infinite degrees of intensity.

22. It is by this principle of combining and attracting that things are brought together. This principle is of universal application and is the sole means whereby the purpose of existence is carried into effect.

23. The expression of growth is met in a most beautiful manner through the instrumentality of this Universal Principle.

24. In order to grow we must obtain what is essential for our growth, but as **we are at all times a complete thought entity**, this completeness makes it possible for us to receive only as we give; **growth is therefore conditioned on reciprocal action**, and we find that on the mental plane

If you desire more financial wealth, ask yourself how much time and effort you spend on consciously and systematically enriching others; where your thoughts, words and actions are not driven by selfish motives, but altruistic ones instead; where your desire is to serve others, so this service can be extended to you, too.

Pay good attention to whom you are mingling with; what language they use; what they do, and how they live. This way you will be able to quickly identify if you should continue seeking their company, or if you rather not spend time seeking those using harmonious thoughts, harmonious language, and expressing themselves in harmonious and mutually enriching and beneficial ways.

Let's take the mobile phone once again: if you weren't interested in its other features, you wouldn't be paying attention to them. Even if you were, there'd still be more that you aren't aware of. Why? No interest, therefore no attention.

like attracts like, that mental vibrations respond only to the extent of their vibratory harmony.

25. It is clear, therefore, that thoughts of abundance will respond only to similar thoughts; the wealth of the individual is seen to be what he inherently is. **Affluence within is found to be the secret of attraction for affluence without**. The ability to produce is found to be the real source of wealth of the individual. It is for this reason that he who has his heart in his work is certain to meet with unbounded success. He will give and continually give; and **the more he gives, the more he will receive**.

26. What do the great financiers of Wall Street, the captains of industry, the statesmen, the great corporation attorneys, the inventors, the physicians, the authors — what do each of these contribute to the sum of human happiness but the power of their thought?

27. Thought is the energy by which the Law of Attraction is brought into operation, which eventually manifests in abundance.

28. **The Universal Mind is static mind or Substance in equilibrium**. It is differentiated into form by our power to think. Thought is the dynamic phase of mind.

29. Power depends upon consciousness of power; unless we use it, we shall lose it, and unless we are conscious of it, we cannot use it.

30. The use of this power depends upon **attention**; the degree of attention determines our capacity for the acquirement of knowledge which is another name for power.

31. Attention has been held to be the distinguishing mark of genius. **The cultivation of attention depends upon practice**.

32. The incentive of attention is interest; the greater the interest, the greater the attention; the greater the attention, the greater the interest, action and reaction; begin by paying attention; before long you will have aroused interest; this interest will attract more attention, and this attention will produce more interest, and so on. This practice will enable you to cultivate the power of attention.

Power depends upon consciousness of power; unless we use it, we shall lose it, and unless we are conscious of it, we cannot use it.

33.   This week concentrate upon your power to create; seek insight, perception; try to find a logical basis for the faith which is in you. Let the thought dwell on the fact that the physical man lives and moves and has his being in the sustainer of all organic life, air, that he must breathe to live. Then let the thought rest on the fact that the spiritual man also lives and moves and has his being in a similar but subtler energy upon which he must depend for life, and that as in the physical world no life assumes form until after a seed is sown, and no higher fruit than that of the parent stock can be produced; so in the spiritual world no effect can be produced until the seed is sown and the fruit will depend upon the nature of the seed, so that **the results which you secure depend upon your perception of law in the mighty domain of causation**, the highest evolution of human consciousness.

"There is no thought in my mind but it quickly tends to convert itself into a power and organizes a huge instrumentality of means."
— RALPH WALDO EMERSON

171. *How is the difference in individual lives measured?*
By the degree of intelligence which they manifest.

172. *What is the law by which the individual may control other forms of intelligence?*
A recognition of the self as an individualization of the Universal Intelligence.

173. *Where does the creative power originate?*
In the Universal.

174. *How does the Universal create form?*
By means of the individual.

175. *What is the connecting link between the individual and the Universal?*
Thought.

176. *What is the principle by which the means of existence is carried into effect?*
The Law of Love.

177. *How is this principle brought into expression?*
By the Law of Growth.

178. *Upon what condition does the Law of Growth depend?*
Upon reciprocal action. The individual is complete at all times and this makes it possible to receive only as we give.

179. *What is it that we give?*
Thought.

180. *What do we receive?*
Thought, which is substance in equilibrium and which is constantly being differentiated in form by what we think.

19

DEVELOPING YOUR VITAL FORCE

Fear is a powerful form of thought. It paralyses the nerve centres, thus affecting the circulation of the blood. This, in turn, paralyses the muscular system, so that fear affects the entire being, body, brain and nerve, physical, mental, and muscular.

Of course the way to overcome fear is to become conscious of power. What is this mysterious vital force which we call power? We do not know, but then, neither do we know what electricity is. But we do know that by conforming to the requirements of the law by which electricity is governed, it will be our obedient servant; that it will light our homes, our cities, run our machinery, and serve us in many useful capacities.

And so it is with vital force. Although we do not know what it is, and possibly may never know, we do know that it is a primary force which manifests through living bodies, and that by complying with the laws and principles by which it is governed, we can open ourselves to a more abundant inflow of this vital energy, and thus express the highest possible degree of mental, moral, and spiritual efficiency.

This part tells of a very simply way of developing this vital force. If you put into practice the information outlined in this lesson you will soon develop the sense of power which has ever been the distinguishing mark of genius.

DEVELOPING YOUR VITAL FORCE

1. The search for truth is no longer a haphazard adventure, but it is a systematic process, and is **logical in its operation**. Every kind of experience is given a voice in shaping its decision.

2. **In seeking the truth we are seeking ultimate cause**; we know that every human experience is an effect; then if we may ascertain the cause, and if we shall find that this cause is one which we can consciously control, the effect or the experience will be within our control also.

3. Human experience will then no longer be the football of fate; a man will not be the child of fortune, but destiny. Fate and

fortune will be controlled as readily as a captain controls his ship, or an engineer his train.

4. All things are finally resolvable into the same element and as they are thus translatable, one into the other, they must ever be in relation and may never be in opposition to one another.

5. In the physical world there are innumerable contrasts, and these may for convenience sake, be designated by distinctive names. There are sizes, colours, shades or ends to all things. There is a North Pole, and a South Pole, an inside and an outside, a seen and an unseen, but these expressions merely serve to place extremes in contrast.

6. They are names given to two different parts of one quantity. The two **extremes are relative**; they are not separate entities, but are two parts or aspects of the whole.

7. In the Mental World we find the same law; we speak of knowledge and ignorance, but ignorance is but a lack of knowledge and is therefore found to be simply a word to express the absence of knowledge; **it has no principle in itself**.

8. In the Moral World we again find the same law; we speak of good and evil, but Good is a reality, something tangible, while Evil is found to be simply a negative condition, the absence of Good. Evil is sometimes thought to be a very real condition, but it has no principle, no vitality, no life; we know this because it can always be destroyed by Good; just as Truth destroys Error and light destroys darkness, so Evil vanishes when Good appears; **there is therefore but one principle in the Moral World**.

9. We find exactly the same law obtaining in the Spiritual World; we speak of mind and matter as two separate entities, but clearer insight makes it evident that there is but one operative principle and that is mind.

10. **Mind is the real and the eternal. Matter is forever changing**; we know that in the aeons of time a hundred years is but as a day. If we stand in any large city and let the eye rest on the innumerable large and magnificent buildings, the vast array of modern automobiles, telephones, the electric lights,

Here's another way of looking at it: Evil aways requires Good in order to fight it, but Good can quite happily exist without Evil. Therefore Evil can never completely remove or conquer Good, for when Good is gone, Evil loses its definition. It would vanish in an instant, as it lacks a vital principle.

Extend this to today's devices, and just remember for a moment what happened to the computer from the 1980s or even most cars from the 1960s. That's a mere half century ago. Now picture where your iPhone® or iPad® or Blackberry® are going to be in 50 years time – or where they were in 1960, a mere 50 years ago.

As an additional exercise, answer yourself the question, what sets today's communication devices apart from those of the 1960s. You will arrive at the answer that it is nothing but the thought of hundreds and thousands of people. In its essence it's once again consciousness that determines real power.

and all the other conveniences of modern civilization, we may remember that not one of them was there just over a century ago, and if we could stand on the same spot in a hundred years from now, in all probability we should find that but few of them remained.

11. In the animal kingdom we find the same law of change. The millions and millions of animals come and go, a few years constituting their span of life. In the plant world the change is still more rapid. Many plants and nearly all grasses come and go in a single year. When we pass to the inorganic, we expect to find something more substantial, but as we gaze on the apparently solid continent, we are told that it arose from the ocean; we see the giant mountain and are told that the place where it now stands was once a lake; and as we stand in awe before the great cliffs in the Yosemite Valley we can easily trace the path of the glaciers which carried all before them.

12. We are in the presence of **continual change**, and we know that this change is but the evolution of the Universal Mind, the grand process whereby all things are continually being created anew, and we come to know that matter is but a form which mind takes and is therefore simply a condition. **Matter has no principle; mind is the only principle**.

13. We have then come to know that mind is the only principle which is operative in the physical, mental, moral and spiritual world.

14. We also know that this mind is static, mind at rest, we also know that the ability of the individual to think is his ability to act upon the Universal Mind and convert it into dynamic mind, or mind in motion.

15. In order to do this fuel must be applied in the form of food, for man cannot think without eating, and so we find that even a spiritual activity such as thinking cannot be converted into sources of pleasure and profit except by making use of material means.

16. It requires energy of some kind to collect electricity and convert it into a dynamic power, it requires the rays of the sun to give the necessary energy to sustain plant life, so it also

requires energy in the form of food to enable the individual to think and thereby act upon the Universal Mind.

17. You may know that thought constantly, eternally is taking form, is forever seeking expression, or you may not, but the fact remains that if your thought is powerful, constructive, and positive, this will be plainly evident in the state of your health, your business and your environment. If your thought is weak, critical, destructive and negative generally, it will manifest in your body as fear, worry and nervousness, in your finance as lack and limitation, and in discordant conditions in your environment.

18. All wealth is the offspring of power; possessions are of value only as they confer power. Events are significant only as they affect power; **all things represent certain forms and degrees of power**.

19. A knowledge of cause and effect as shown by the laws governing steam, electricity, chemical affinity and gravitation enables men to plan courageously and to execute fearlessly. These laws are called Natural Laws, because they govern the physical world, but all power is not physical power; there is also mental power, and there is moral and spiritual power.

20. What are our schools, our universities, but mental power-houses, places where mental power is being developed?

21. As there are many mighty powerhouses for the application of power to ponderous machinery, whereby raw material is collected and converted into the necessities and comforts of life, so the mental powerhouses collect the raw material and cultivate and develop it into a power which is infinitely superior to all the forces of nature, marvellous though they may be.

22. What is this raw material which is being collected in these thousands of mental powerhouses all over the world and developed into a power which is evidently controlling every other power? In its static form it is **mind** – in its dynamic form, it is **thought**.

23. **This power is superior because it exists on a higher plane**, because it has enabled man to discover the law by

which these wonderful forces of Nature could be harnessed and made to do the work of hundreds and thousands of men. It has enabled man to discover laws whereby time and space have been annihilated, and the law of gravitation overcome.

24. Thought is the vital force or energy which is being developed and which has produced such startling results in the last half century as to bring about a world which would be absolutely inconceivable to a man existing only 50 or 25 years ago. If such results have been secured by organizing these mental powerhouses in 50 years, what may not be expected in another 50 years?

See my comments on the previous page. In fact all of the modern devices we use today were (!) inconceivable 50 years ago, otherwise they would have been conceived. That said, they certainly did lay the foundation for whatever followed.

25. The substance from which all things are created is infinite in quantity; we know that light travels at the rate of 186,000 miles per second, and we know that there are stars so remote that it takes light 2,000 years to reach us, and we know that such stars exist in all parts of the heaven; we know, too, that this light comes in waves, so that if the **ether** on which these waves travel was not continuous, the light would fail to reach us; we can then only come to the conclusion that this substance, or ether, or raw material, is universally present.

What was then called 'ether', we now call the Zero Point Field or the Universal Consciousness. Back then it was believed it to be some substance, whereas now we regard it as pure consciousness, so fine and subtle that it permeates all things.

26. How, then, does it manifest in form? In electrical science a battery is formed by connecting the opposite poles of zinc and copper, which causes a current to flow from one to the other and so provides energy. This same process is repeated in respect to every polarity, and as **all form simply depends upon the rate of vibration** and consequent relations of atoms to each other, if we wish to change the form of manifestation we must change the polarity. This is the **Principle of Causation.**

...which is another of the seven Hermetic Principles. You can read more about them in the "Kybalion", which is also a free download on masterkeysystem.tv.

27. For your exercise this week, concentrate, and when I use the word concentrate, I mean all that the word implies; **become so absorbed in the object of your thought that you are conscious of nothing else**, and do this a few minutes every day. You take the necessary time to eat in order that the body may be nourished, why not take the time to assimilate your mental food?

28. Let the thought rest on the fact that appearances are deceptive. The Earth is not flat, neither is it stationary; the sky is

not a dome, the Sun does not move, the stars are not small specks of light, and matter which was once supposed to be fixed has been found to be in a state of perpetual flux.

29. Try to realize that the day is fast approaching — its dawn is now at hand — when modes of thought and action must be adjusted to rapidly increasing knowledge of the operation of eternal principles.

"The power to think consecutively and deeply and clearly, is an avowed and deadly enemy to mistakes and blunders, super- stitions, unscientific theories, irrational beliefs, unbridled enthusiasm, fanaticism."
— HADDOCK

181. *How are extremes placed in contrast?*
They are designated by distinctive names, such as inside and outside, top and bottom, light and dark, good and bad.

182. *Are these separate entities?*
No, they are parts or aspects of one Whole.

183. *What is the one creative Principle in the physical, mental and spiritual world?*
The Universal Mind, or the Eternal Energy from which all things proceed.

184. *How are we related to this creative Principle?*
By our ability to think.

185. *How does this creative Principle become operative?*
Thought is the seed, which results in action and action results in form.

186. *Upon what does form depend?*
Upon the rate of vibration.

187. *How may the rate of vibration be changed?*
By mental action.

188. *Upon what does mental action depend?*
Upon polarity, action and reaction, between the individual and the Universal.

189. *Does the creative energy originate in the individual or the Universal?*
In the Universal, but the Universal can manifest only through the individual.

190. *Why is the individual necessary?*
Because the Universal is static, and requires energy to start it in motion. This is furnished by food which is converted into energy, which in turn enables the individual to think. When the individual stops eating, he stops thinking; then he no longer acts upon the Universal; there is consequently no longer any action or reaction; the Universal is then only pure mind in static form — mind at rest.

20

THINKING AS THE TRUE BUSINESS IN LIFE

For many years there has been an endless discussion as to the origin of evil. Theologians have told us that God is Love, and that God is omnipresent. If this be true, there is no place where God is not. Where, then, is Evil, Satan and Hell? Let us see:

- God is Spirit.
- Spirit is the Creative Principle of the Universe.
- Man is made in the image and likeness of God.
- Man is therefore a spiritual being.
- The only activity which spirit possesses is the power to think.
- Thinking is therefore a creative process.
- All form is therefore the result of the thinking process.
- The destruction of form must also be a result of the thinking process.
- Fictitious representations of form are the result of the creative power of thought, as in (Stage-) Hypnotism.
- Apparent representation of form are the result of the creative power of thought, as in Spiritualism.
- Invention, organization and constructive work of all kinds are the result of the creative power of thought, as in Concentration.

When the creative power of thought is manifested for the benefit of humanity, we call the result good.

When the creative power of thought is manifested in a destructive or evil manner, we call the result evil.

This indicates the origin of both good and evil; they are simply words which have been coined in order to indicate the nature of the result of the thinking or creative process.

Thought necessarily precedes and predetermines action; action precedes and predetermines condition.

Part Twenty will throw more light upon this important subject.

THINKING AS THE TRUE BUSINESS IN LIFE

I. The spirit of a thing is that thing; it is necessarily fixed, changeless and eternal. The spirit of you is — you; without

The secret of power is a perfect understanding of the principles, forces, methods and combinations of Mind, and a perfect understanding of our relationship to the Universal Mind.

the spirit you would be nothing. It becomes active through your recognition of it and its possibilities.

2. You may have all the wealth in Christendom, but unless you recognize it and make use of it, it will have no value; so with your spiritual wealth: unless you recognize it and use it, it will have no value. **The one and only condition of spiritual power is use or recognition**.

3. All great things come through recognition; the sceptre of power is consciousness, and thought is its messenger, and this messenger is constantly moulding the realities of the invisible world into the conditions and environments of your objective world.

4. Thinking is the true business of life, power is the result. You are at all times dealing with the magical power of thought and consciousness. What results can you expect so long as you remain oblivious to the power which has been placed within your control?

5. So long as you do this you limit yourself to superficial conditions, and make of yourself a beast of burden for those who think; those who recognize their power; those who know that unless we are willing to think we shall have to work, and the less we think the more we shall have to work, and the less we shall get for our work.

6. The secret of power is a perfect understanding of the principles, forces, methods and combinations of mind, and a perfect understanding of our relationship to the Universal Mind. It is well to remember that this principle is unchangeable; if this were not so, it would not be reliable; all principles are changeless.

7. This **stability** is your opportunity; you are its active attribute, the channel for its activity; the Universal can act only through the individual.

8. When you begin to perceive that the essence of the Universal is within yourself — is you — you begin to do things; **you begin to feel your power**; it is the fuel which fires the imagination; which lights the torch of inspiration; which gives vitality to thought; which enables you to connect with all the invisible forces of the Universe. It is this power which will enable you to plan fearlessly, to execute masterfully.

9. But perception will come only in the Silence; this seems to be the condition required for all great purposes. You are a visualizing entity. Imagination is your workshop. It is here that your ideal is to be visualized.

10. As a perfect understanding of the nature of this power is a primary condition for its manifestation, visualize the entire method over and over again, so that you may use it whenever occasion requires. The infinity of wisdom is to follow the method whereby we may have the inspiration of the omnipotent Universal Mind on demand at any time.

11. We can fail to recognize this world within, and so exclude it from our consciousness, but it will still be the basic fact of all existence; and when we learn to recognize it, not only in ourselves, but in all persons, events, things and circumstances we shall have found the »Kingdom of Heaven« which we are told is »within« us.

12. Our failures are a result of the operation of exactly the same principle; the principle is unchangeable; its operation is exact, there is no deviation; if we think lack, limitation, discord, we shall find their fruits on every hand; if we think poverty, unhappiness or disease, the thought messengers will carry the summons as readily as any other kind of thought and the result will be just as certain. If we fear a coming calamity, we shall be able to say with Job, »the thing I feared has come upon me«; if we think unkindly or ignorantly we shall thus attract to ourselves the results of our ignorance.

13. This power of thought, if understood and correctly used, is the greatest labour-saving device ever dreamed of, **but if**

"Kingdom of Heaven" is a reference to Luke 17:21. Interesting in this light are also the following passages 17:24 and 17:26, which, depending on which bible "translation" one gives credence, could lead to rather different interpretations. One (English Standard Version ©2001) speaks of the Son of Man as a new "enlightened" being. Another one (New International Version ©1984) could be interpreted as the Son of Man being the dire consequences of our very own thinking, feeling, speaking and doing, resulting in the cataclysmic changes that many ancient prophecies speak of.

not understood or improperly used, the result will in all probability be disastrous, as we have already seen. By the help of this power you can confidently undertake things that are seemingly impossible, because this power is the secret of all inspiration, all genius.

14. **To become inspired means to get out of the beaten path**, out of the rut, because extraordinary results require extraordinary means. When we come into a recognition of the Unity of all things and that the source of all power is within, we tap the source of inspiration.

15. Inspiration is the art of imbibing, the art of self-realization; the art of adjusting the individual mind to that of the Universal Mind; **the art of attaching the proper mechanism to the source of all power**; the art of differentiating the formless into form; the art of becoming a channel for the flow of Infinite Wisdom; the art of visualizing perfection; the art of realizing the omnipresence of Omnipotence.

16. An understanding and appreciation of the fact that the Infinite Power is omnipresent and is therefore in the infinitely small as well as the infinitely large will enable us to absorb its essence. A further understanding of the fact that **this power is Spirit and therefore indivisible** will enable us to appreciate its presence at all points at the same time.

17. An understanding of these facts, first intellectually and then emotionally, will enable us to drink deeply from this ocean of infinite power. An intellectual understanding will be of no assistance; the emotions must be brought into action; thought without feeling is cold. **The required combination is thought and feeling**.

18. Inspiration is from within. The Silence is necessary, the senses must be stilled, the muscles relaxed, repose cultivated. When you have thus come into possession of a sense of poise and power, you will be ready to receive the information or inspiration or wisdom which may be necessary for the development of your purpose.

19. Do not confuse these methods with those of the clairvoyant; they have nothing in common. **Inspiration is the art of receiving** and makes for all that is best in life; your busi-

Those of you more intellectually inclined may ask how to bring in feeling. One way of doing this is to eat or drink something with intent. The moment you swallow it, you feel this intent in your body by the food or drink sliding down the oesophagus. Another one is causeless dancing or any other conscious physical movement as an expression of your joy or fulfilment. The result of that is gratitude.

223

ness in life is to understand and command these invisible forces instead of letting them command and rule you. **Power implies service**; inspiration implies power; to understand and apply the method of inspiration is to become a superman.

Franz Bardon, a German Occultist and Hermetic, suggested to pick out one particular intent at meal time and dedicate every spoon or sip you take to this intent, thus invoking intention, attention, energy and eventually manifestation.

20. **We can live more abundantly every time we breathe, if we consciously breathe with that intention**. The IF is a very important condition in this case, as the intention governs the attention, and without the attention you can secure only the results which every one else secures. That is, a supply equal to the demand.

21. In order to secure the larger supply **your demand must be increased**, and as you consciously increase the demand the supply will follow, you will find yourself coming into a larger and larger supply of life, energy and vitality.

22. The reason for this is not difficult to understand, but it is another of the vital mysteries of life which does not seem to be generally appreciated. If you make it your own, you will find it one of the great realities of life.

A reference to the Bible, Acts 17:28.

In his book, "*The Amazing Secrets of the Yogi*", Charles Haanel offers the reader several Yogic breathing techniques to alleviate ailments and to increase the level of vitality. You will also find many a useful video on sites like Youtube. You may of course also join a Yoga Studio nearby.

23. We are told that »In Him we live and move and have our being,« and we are told that »He« is a Spirit, and again that »He« is Love, so that **every time we breathe, we breathe this life, love, and spirit**. This is Pranic Energy, or Pranic Ether, we could not exist a moment without it. It is the Cosmic Energy; it is the Life of the Solar Plexus.

24. Every time we breathe we fill our lungs with air and at the same time vitalize our body with this Pranic Ether which is Life itself, so that **we have the opportunity of making a conscious connection with All Life, All Intelligence and All Substance**.

Your business in life is to understand and command these invisible forces instead of letting them command and rule you.

You may use thought constructively or destructively, but the immutable law will not allow you to plant a thought of one kind and reap the fruit of another.

25. A knowledge of your relation and oneness with this Principle that governs the Universe, and the simple method whereby you can consciously identify yourself with it, gives you a scientific understanding of a law whereby you may free yourself from disease, from lack or limitation of any kind; in fact, it enables you to breathe the »Breath of Life« into your own nostrils.

A reference to Genesis 2:7.

26. This »Breath of Life« is a superconscious reality. **It is the essence of the »I AM.«** It is **pure »Being«** or **Universal Substance**, and our conscious unity with it enables us to localize it, and thus exercise the powers of this creative energy.

Whenever you formulate an affirmation, always formulate it in the present tense, "I am", or - better still - "We are". You have learned in Part 9 that whatever you desire for yourself, you should affirm for others, too, and it will help you both, for thought is an intelligent power.

27. Thought is creative vibration and the quality of the conditions created will depend upon the quality of our thought, because we cannot express powers which we do not possess. **We must »be« before we can »do«, and we can »do« only to the extent to which we »are«, so what we do will necessarily coincide with what we »are«, and what we »are« depends upon what we »think.«**

28. Every time you think you start a train of causation which will create a condition in strict accordance with the quality of the thought which originated it. Thought which is in harmony with the Universal Mind will result in corresponding conditions. Thought which is destructive or discordant will produce corresponding results. **You may use thought constructively or destructively, but the immutable law will not allow you to plant a thought of one kind and reap the fruit of another**. You are free to use this marvellous creative power as you will, but you must take the consequences.

All this is again subject to law, namely all the 7 Hermetic Principles combined. It is once again us – and only us – who can prevent the latter from happening. Prophecy is not about what is going to happen, but what will happen if one particular path is being favoured over another. With the Master Key System you learn to take the true path. This path will help you even in times of turmoil, which the Earth has seen many times before in its existence, and will see again.

29. This is the danger from what is called »Will Power«. There are those who seem to think that by force of will they can coerce this law; that they can sow seed of one kind and by »Will Power« make it bear fruit of another. However, the fundamental principle of creative power is in the Universal, and therefore the idea of forcing a compliance with our wishes by the power of the individual will is an inverted conception which may appear to succeed for a while, but is eventually doomed to failure – because it antagonizes the very power which it is seeking to use.

30. It is the individual attempting to coerce the Universal, the finite in conflict with the Infinite. Our permanent well being will be best conserved by a **conscious cooperation with the continuous forward movement of the Great Whole**.

31. For your exercise this week, go into the Silence and concentrate on the fact that »In him we live and move and have our being« is literally and scientifically exact! That you ARE because He IS, that if He is Omnipresent He must be in you. That if He is all in all you must be in Him! That He is Spirit and you are made in »His image and likeness«, and that the only difference between His spirit and your spirit is one of degree; that a part must be the same in kind and quality as the whole. When you can realize this clearly, you will have found the secret of the creative power of thought; you will have found the origin of both good and evil; you will have found the secret of the wonderful power of concentration; **you will have found the key to the solution of every problem whether physical, financial, or environmental**.

PART TWENTY — QUESTIONS AND ANSWERS

191. *Upon what condition does power depend?*
Upon recognition and use.

192. *What is recognition?*
Consciousness.

193. *How do we become conscious of power?*
By thinking.

194. *What then is the true business of life?*
Correct scientific thinking.

195. *What is correct scientific thinking?*
The ability to adjust our thought processes to the will of the Universal. In other words, to cooperate with natural laws.

196. *How is this accomplished?*
By securing a perfect understanding of the principles, forces, methods and combinations of mind.

197. *What is this Universal Mind?*
The basic fact of all existence.

198. *What is the cause of all lack, limitation, disease and discord?*
It is due to the operation of exactly the same law, the law operates relentlessly and is continually bringing about conditions in correspondence with the thought which originated or created them.

199. *What is inspiration?*
The art of realizing the omnipresence of Omniscience.

200. *Upon what does the conditions with which we meet depend?*
Upon the quality of our thought. Because what we do depends upon what we are and what we are depends upon what we think.

21

THINKING BIG THOUGHTS AS THE SECRET OF SUCCESS

It is my privilege to enclose Part Twenty-One. In paragraph 7 you will find that one of the secrets of success, one of the methods of organizing victory, **one of the accomplishments of the Master Mind is to think big thoughts**.

In paragraph 8 you will find that everything which we hold in our consciousness for any length of time becomes impressed upon our Subconscious and so becomes a pattern which the creative energy will weave into our life and environment. This is the secret of the wonderful power of prayer.

We know that the Universe is governed by law; that for every effect there must be a cause, and that **the same cause, under the same conditions, will invariably produce the same effect**. Consequently, if prayer has ever been answered, it will always be answered, if the proper conditions are complied with. This must necessarily be true; otherwise the Universe would be a Chaos instead of a Cosmos. The answer to prayer is therefore subject to law, and this law is definite, exact and scientific, just as are the laws governing gravitation and electricity. An understanding of this law takes the foundation of Christianity out of the realm of superstition and credulity and places it upon the firm rock of scientific understanding.

But, unfortunately, there are comparatively few persons who know how to pray. They understand that there are laws governing electricity, mathematics, and chemistry, but, for some inexplicable reason, it never seems to occur to them that there are also spiritual laws, and that these laws are also definite, scientific, exact, and operate with immutable precision.

THINKING BIG THOUGHTS AS THE SECRET OF SUCCESS

I.   The real secret of power is consciousness of power. The Universal Mind is unconditional; therefore, the more conscious we become of our unity with this mind, the less conscious we shall become of conditions and limitations, and as we become emancipated or freed from conditions we come into a realization of the unconditional. We have become free!

The more conscious we become of our unity with the source of all power, the greater will be our power to control and master every condition.

2. As soon as we become conscious of the inexhaustible power in the world within, we begin to draw on this power, and apply and develop the greater possibilities which this discernment has realized, because whatever we become conscious of is invariably manifested in the objective world, is brought forth into tangible expression.

3. This is because the Infinite Mind, which is the source from which all things proceed, is one and indivisible, and each individual is a channel whereby this Eternal Energy is being manifested. Our ability to think is our ability to act upon this Universal substance, and what **we think is what is created or produced in the objective world**.

4. The result of this discovery is nothing less than marvellous, and means that **mind is extraordinary in quality, limitless in quantity, and contains possibilities without number**. To become conscious of this power is to become a »live wire«; it has the same effect as placing an ordinary wire in contact with a wire that is charged. The Universal is the live wire. It carries power sufficient to meet every situation which may arise in the life of every individual. When the individual mind touches the Universal Mind, it receives all the power it requires. **This is the world within**. All science recognizes the reality of this world, and **all power is contingent upon our recognition of this world**.

5. The ability to eliminate imperfect conditions depends upon mental action, and mental action depends upon consciousness of power; therefore, the more conscious we become of our unity with the source of all power, the greater will be our power to control and master every condition.

6. **Large ideas have a tendency to eliminate all smaller ideas**, so that it is well to hold ideas large enough to coun-

231

teract and destroy all small or undesirable tendencies. This will remove innumerable petty and annoying obstacles from your path. You also **become conscious of a larger world of thought**, thereby increasing your mental capacity as well as placing yourself in position to accomplish something of value.

7. This is one of the secrets of success, one of the methods of organizing victory, one of the accomplishments of the Master Mind: he thinks big thoughts. The creative energies of mind find no more difficulty in handling large situations, than small ones. Mind is just as much present in the infinitely large as in the infinitely small.

8. When we realize these facts concerning mind, we understand how we may bring to ourselves any condition **by creating the corresponding conditions in our consciousness**, because everything which is held for any length of time in the consciousness, eventually becomes impressed upon the Subconscious and thus becomes a pattern which the creative energy will weave into the life and environment of the individual.

9. In this way conditions are produced and we find that our lives are simply the reflection of our predominant thoughts, our mental attitude. We see then that the science of correct thinking is the one science – that it includes all other sciences.

10. From this science we learn that every thought creates an impression on the brain, that these impressions create mental tendencies, and these tendencies create character, ability and purpose, and that **the combined action of character, ability and purpose determines the experiences with which we shall meet in life**.

11. These experiences come to us through the Law of Attraction; through the action of this law we meet in the world without the experiences which correspond to our world within.

12. The predominant thought or the mental attitude is the magnet, and the law is that »like attracts like«, consequently the mental attitude will invariably attract such conditions as correspond to its nature.

The real secret is our understanding of who we really are, and subsequently the application of techniques like meditation and concentration, that lead to an actual physical change of both brain and body tissue and to therefore the complete reinvention of ourselves as Human Beings.

Impress on the mind a perfect picture of the desire which you wish to have objectified and continue to hold the picture in mind until results are obtained.

13. This mental attitude is our personality and is composed of the thoughts which we have been creating in our own mind; therefore, if we wish a change in conditions all that is necessary is to change our thought; this will in turn change our mental attitude, which will in turn change our personality, which will in turn change the persons, things and conditions, or, the experiences with which we meet in life.

14. It is, however, no easy matter to change the mental attitude, but by **persistent effort** it may be accomplished; the mental attitude is patterned after the mental pictures which have been photographed on the brain. If you do not like the pictures, destroy the negatives and create new pictures; this is the art of visualization.

15. As soon as you have done this you will begin to attract new things, and the new things will correspond to the new pictures. To do this, impress on the mind a perfect picture of the desire which you wish to have objectified and continue to hold the picture in mind until results are obtained.

16. If the desire is one which requires determination, ability, talent, courage, power or any other spiritual power, these are necessary essentials for your picture; build them in; they are the vital part of the picture; they are the feeling which combines with thought and creates the irresistible magnetic power which draws the things you require to you. They give your picture life, and life means growth, and as soon as it begins to grow, the result is practically assured.

17. **Do not hesitate to aspire to the highest possible attainments in anything you may undertake**, for the mind forces are ever ready to lend themselves to a purposeful will

Dare to believe in your own idea; remember that Nature is plastic to the ideal; think of the ideal as an already accomplished fact.

Neale Donald Walsch put it nicely in "Conversations with God", where God answered upon his question, how to stop smoking: "Stop smoking!" It really is that simple, but it has to be done, not just thought about or affirmed. Equally, you can analyze to death whatever undesirable trait or habit you have, fact is that you have to move over to the other side, read: set a new cause, if you ever want to experience a different result.

Albert Einstein is quoted saying: "*We cannot solve the problem with the same kind of thinking that created it in the first place.*" The same applies to us, too. A new kind thinking is necessary, and a new courage to tackle ideals and dreams and bring them to fruition. With our recognition of the omnipresence of the Omniscient, this should by now be an easy task for you.

"Only see the world without..." This is especially true for those who analyze existing, undesirable situations, while forgetting that as long as they do this, a desirable situation cannot be given birth to. It is law that you have to set a new cause, if you want a new effect. As long as you know that this situation is undesirable, you can give thanks for it showing up in your life, for it taught you where you don't want to be. Then move over to the other side and never look back. Do this every time such situations emerge. Give thanks, forgive, love and let go!

in the effort to crystallize its highest aspirations into acts, accomplishments, and events.

18. An illustration of how these mind forces operate is suggested by the method in which all our habits are formed. We do a thing, then do it again, and again, and again, until it becomes easy and perhaps almost automatic; and the same rule applies in breaking any and all bad habits; we stop doing a thing, and then avoid it again, and again until we are entirely free from it; and if we do fail now and then, we should by no means lose hope, for the law is absolute and invincible and gives us credit for every effort and every success, even though our efforts and successes are perhaps intermittent.

19. There is no limit to what this law can do for you; dare to believe in your own idea; remember that Nature is plastic to the ideal; think of the ideal as an already accomplished fact.

20. **The real battle of life is one of ideas; it is being fought out by the few against the many**; on the one side is the constructive and creative thought, on the other side the destructive and negative thought; the creative thought is dominated by an ideal, the passive thought is dominated by appearances. On both sides are men of science, men of letters, and men of affairs.

21. On the creative side are men who spend their time in laboratories, or over microscopes and telescopes, side by side with the men who dominate the commercial, political, and scientific world; on the negative side or men who spend their time investigating law and precedent, men who mistake theology for religion, statesmen who mistake might for right, and all the millions who seem to prefer precedent to progress, who are eternally looking backward instead of forward, who see only the world without, but know nothing of the world within.

22. In the last analysis there are but these two classes; all men will have to take their place on one side or the other; they will have to go forward, or go back. There is no standing still in a world where all is motion; it is this attempt to stand still that gives sanction and force to arbitrary and unequal codes of law.

23. That we are in a period of transition is evidenced by the unrest which is everywhere apparent. The complaint of humanity is as a roll of heaven's artillery, commencing with low and threatening notes and increasing until the sound is sent from cloud to cloud, and the lightning splits the air and Earth.

24. The sentries who patrol the most advanced outposts of the Industrial, Political, and Religious world are calling anxiously to each other. What of the night? The danger and insecurity of the position they occupy and attempt to hold is becoming more apparent every hour. The dawn of a new era necessarily declares that the existing order of things cannot much longer be.

25. The issue between the old regime and the new, the crux of the social problem, is entirely a question of conviction in the minds of the people as to the nature of the Universe. When they realize that the transcendent force of spirit or mind of the Cosmos is within each individual, it will be possible to frame laws that shall consider the liberties and rights of the many instead of the privileges of the few.

26. As long as the people regard the Cosmic Power as a power nonhuman and alien to humanity, so long will it be comparatively easy for a supposed privileged class to rule by Divine right in spite of every protest of social sentiment. **The real interest of democracy is therefore to exalt, emancipate and recognize the divinity of the human spirit**; to recognize that all power is from within; that no human being has any more power than any other human being, except such as may willingly be delegated to him. The old regime would have us believe that the law was superior to the law-makers. Herein is the gist of the social crime of every form of privilege and

Silent thought concentration is therefore the true method of reaching, awakening, and then expressing the wonderful potential power of the world within.

personal inequality, the institutionalising of the fatalistic doctrine of Divine election.

27. The Divine Mind is the Universal Mind; it makes no exceptions, it plays no favourites; it does not act through sheer caprice or from anger, jealousy or wrath; neither can it be flattered, cajoled or moved by sympathy or petition to supply man with some need which he thinks necessary for his happiness or even his existence. **The Divine Mind makes no exceptions in favour any individual**; but when the individual understands and realizes his Unity with the Universal principle he will appear to be favoured because he will have found the source of all health, all wealth, and all power.

28. For your exercise this week, **concentrate on the Truth**. Try to realize that the Truth shall make you free, that is, nothing can permanently stand in the way of your perfect success when you learn to apply the scientifically correct thought methods and principles. Realize that you are externalising in your environment your inherent soul potencies. Realize that the Silence offers an ever available and almost unlimited opportunity for awakening the highest conception of Truth. Try to comprehend that Omnipotence itself is absolute silence, all else is change, activity, limitation. Silent thought concentration is therefore the true method of reaching, awakening, and then expressing the wonderful potential power of the world within.

"The possibilities of thought training are infinite, its consequence eternal, and yet few take the pains to direct their thinking into channels that will do them good, but instead leave all to chance."
— BRICE MARDEN

237

This is the true essence of all the weeks of studying. Without consciousness, there's no manifestation. All that you become conscious of will find its way into your Being by means of your senses – the process of noticing external things which had their cause set in the past, and with which you are into resonance – consciously or subconsciously. If you don't like what you perceive through your senses, think again - and differently - and set in motion an entirely new chain of causation, which has to result in corresponding effects.

201. *What is the real secret of power?*
The consciousness of power, because whatever we become conscious of, is invariably manifested in the objective world, is brought forth into tangible expression.

202. *What is the source of this power?*
The Universal Mind, from which all things proceed, and which is one and indivisible.

203. *How is this power being manifested?*
Through the individual, each individual is a channel whereby this energy is being differentiated in form.

204. *How may we connect with this Omnipotence?*
Our ability to think is our ability to act on this Universal Energy, and what we think is what is produced or created in the objective world.

205. *What is the result of this discovery?*
The result is nothing less than marvellous, it opens unprecedented and limitless opportunity.

206. *How, then, may we eliminate imperfect conditions?*
By becoming conscious of our Unity with the source of all power.

207. *What is one of the distinctive characteristics of the Master Mind?*
He thinks big thoughts, he holds ideas large enough to counteract and destroy all petty and annoying obstacles.

208. *How do experiences come to us?*
Through the Law of Attraction.

209. *How is this law brought into operation?*
By our predominant mental attitude.

210. *What is the issue between the old regime and the new?*
A question of conviction as to the nature of the Universe. The old regime is trying to cling to the fatalistic doctrine of Divine election. The new regime recognizes the divinity of the individual, the democracy of humanity.

22

NEW THINKING, NEW MAN

In Part Twenty-two you will find that thoughts are spiritual seeds, which, when planted in the Subconscious Mind, have a tendency to sprout and grow, but unfortunately the fruit is frequently not to our liking.

The various forms of inflammation, paralysis, nervousness and diseased conditions generally, are the manifestation of fear, worry, care, anxiety, jealousy, hatred and similar thought.

The life processes are carried on by two distinct methods; first, the taking up and making use of nutritive material necessary for constructing cells; second, breaking down and excreting the waste material.

All life is based upon these constructive and destructive activities, and as food, water and air are the only requisites necessary for the construction of cells, it would seem that the problem of prolonging life indefinitely would not be a very difficult one.

However strange it may seem, it is the second or destructive activity that is, with rare exception, the cause of all disease. The waste material accumulates and saturates the tissues, which causes autointoxication. This may be partial or general. In the first case the disturbance will be local; in the second place it will affect the whole system.

The problem, then, before us in the healing of disease is **to increase the inflow and distribution of vital energy throughout the system**, and this can only be done by eliminating thoughts of fear, worry, care, anxiety, jealousy, hatred, and every other destructive thought, which tend to tear down and destroy the nerves and glands which control the excretion and elimination of poisonous and waste matter.

»Nourishing foods and strengthening tonics« cannot bestow life, because these are but secondary manifestations to life. The primary manifestation of life and how you may get in touch with it is explained in the Part which I have the privilege of enclosing herewith.

NEW THINKING, NEW MAN

1. Knowledge is of priceless value, because by applying knowledge we can make our future what we wish it to be. When we realize that our present character, our present environment, our present ability, our present physical condition are **all the result of past methods of thinking**, we shall begin to have some conception of the value of knowledge.

2. If the state of our health is not all that could be desired, let us examine our method of thinking; let us remember that every thought produces an impression on the mind; **every impression is a seed which will sink into the Subconscious** and form a tendency; the tendency will be to attract other similar thoughts and before we know it we shall have a crop which must be harvested.

3. If these thoughts contain disease germs, the harvest will be sickness, decay, weakness, and failure; the question is, what are we thinking, what are we creating, what is the harvest to be?

4. If there is any physical condition which it is necessary to change, the law governing visualization will be found effective. Make a mental image of physical perfection; hold it in the mind until it is absorbed by the consciousness. Many have eliminated chronic ailments in a few weeks by this method, and thousands have overcome and destroyed all manner of ordinary physical disturbances by this method in a few days, sometimes in a few minutes.

5. It is through the **Law of Vibration** that the mind exercises this control over the body. We know that **every mental action is a vibration**, and we know that **all form is simply a mode of motion**, a rate of vibration. Therefore, any given

Vibration is another of the
7 Hermetic Principles, which are:

1. Mentality
2. Correspondence
3. Vibration
4. Rhythm
5. Polarity
6. Cause and Effect
7. Gender

All of them have been dealt with over the past weeks. Gender may not be so obvious, but it is displayed through Positive and Negative, whereby the Positive gives the impulse, and the Negative receives it. For you it means that there's a time when you have to set the impulse and move forward, and a time when you step back and consciously become aware of your environment, absorb new information, process it, classify and order it, so that you gain additional certainty, centeredness and peace of mind. This allows you to move forward with ease, accomplish things, get stuff done, and thus achieve your goals.

Make a mental image of physical perfection; hold it in the mind until it is absorbed by the consciousness.

vibration immediately modifies every atom in the body, every life cell is affected and an entire chemical change is made in every group of life cells.

6. **Everything in the Universe is what it is by virtue of its rate of vibration**. Change the rate of vibration and you change the nature, quality and form. The vast panorama of nature, both visible and invisible, is being constantly changed by simply changing the rate of vibration, and as thought is a vibration we can also exercise this power. We can change the vibration and thus produce any condition which we desire to manifest in our bodies.

7. We are all using this power every minute. The trouble is most of us are using it unconsciously and thus producing undesirable results. The challenge is to use it intelligently and produce only desirable results. This should not be difficult, because we all have had sufficient experience to know what produces pleasant vibration in the body, and we also know the causes which produce the unpleasant and disagreeable sensations.

8. All that is necessary is to consult our own experience. When our thought has been uplifted, progressive, constructive, courageous, noble, kind or in any other way desirable, we have set in motion vibrations which brought about certain results. When our thought has been filled with envy, hatred, jealousy, criticism or any of the other thousand and one forms of discord, certain vibrations were set in motion which brought about certain other results of a different nature, and each of these rates of vibration, if kept up, crystallized in form. In the first case the result was mental, moral and physical health, and in the second case discord, inharmony and disease.

9. We can understand, then, something of the power which the mind possesses over the body.

10. The Subjective Mind has certain effects on the body which are readily recognized. Someone says something to you which strikes you as ludicrous and you laugh, possibly until your whole body shakes, which shows that thought has control over the muscles of your body; or someone says something which excites your sympathy and your eyes fill with tears,

which shows that thought controls the glands of your body; or someone says something which makes you angry and the blood mounts to your cheek, which shows that thought controls the circulation of your blood. But as these experiences are all the results of the action of your Subjective Mind over the body, **the results are of a temporary nature**; they soon pass away and leave the situation as it was before.

11.   Let us see how the action of the Subconscious Mind over the body differs. You receive a wound; thousands of cells being the work of healing at once; in a few days or a few weeks the work is complete. You may even break a bone. No surgeon on Earth can weld the parts together (I am not referring to the insertion of rods or other devices to strengthen or replace bones). He may set the bone for you, and the Subjective Mind will immediately begin the process of welding the parts together, and in a short time the bone is as solid as it ever was. You may swallow poison; the Subjective Mind will immediately discover the danger and make violent efforts to eliminate it. You may become infected with a dangerous germ; the Subjective Mind will at once commence to build a wall around the infected area and destroy the infection by absorbing it in the white blood corpuscles which it supplies for the purpose.

12.   **These processes of the Subconscious Mind usually proceed without our personal knowledge or direction**, and so long as we do not interfere the result is perfect, but, as these millions of repair cells are all intelligent and respond to our thought, they are often paralysed and rendered impotent by our thoughts of fear, doubt, and anxiety. They are like an army of workmen, ready to start an important piece of work, but every time they get started on the undertaking a strike is called, or plans changed, until they finally get discouraged and give up.

13.   The way to health is founded on the Law of Vibration, which is the basis of all science, and this law is brought into operation by the mind, the »world within.« **It is a matter of individual effort and practice**. Our world of power is within; if we are wise we shall not waste time and effort in trying to deal with

effects as we find them in the »world without,« which is only an external, **a reflection**.

It should rather say: "ONLY by changing the cause, we change the effect", for – as mentioned above – far too many people are still only dealing with the effects in the world without, but are entirely ignorant of the causes that have to be set in the world within.

14. We shall always find the cause in the »world within«; by changing the cause, we change the effect.

15. Every cell in your body is intelligent and will respond to your direction. The cells are all creators and will create the exact pattern which you give them.

16. Therefore, when perfect images are placed before the subjective, the creative energies will build a perfect body.

17. Brain cells are constructed in the same way. The quality of the brain is governed by the state of mind, or mental attitude, so that if undesirable mental attitudes are conveyed to the subjective they will in turn be transferred to the body; we can therefore readily see that if we wish the body to manifest health, strength and vitality this must be the predominant thought.

18. We know then that every element of the human body is the result of a rate of vibration.

19. We know that mental action is a rate of vibration.

20. We know that **a higher rate of vibration governs, modifies, controls, changes, or destroys a lower rate of vibration**.

21. We know that the rate of vibration is governed by the character of brain cells, and finally,

22. We know how to create these brain cells; therefore,

23. We know how to make any physical change in the body we desire, and having secured a working knowledge of the power of mind to this extent. We have come to know that there is practically no limitation which can be placed upon our ability to place ourselves in harmony with Natural Law, which is omnipotent.

24. This influence or control over the body by mind is coming to be more and more generally understood, and many physi-

We shall always find the cause in the »world within«; by changing the cause, we change the effect.

cians are now giving the matter their earnest attention. Dr. Albert T. Schofield, who has written several important books on the subject, say, »The subject of mental therapeutics is still ignored in medical works generally. In our physiologies no references is made to the central controlling power that rules the body for its good, and the power of the mind over the body is seldom spoken of«.

25. No doubt many physicians treat nervous diseases of functional origin wisely and well, but what we contend is that the knowledge they display was taught at no school, was learned from no book, but it is intuitive and empirical.

26. This is not as it should be. The power of **mental therapeutics** should be the subject of careful, special and scientific teaching in every medical school. We might pursue the subject of maltreatment, or want of treatment, further in detail and describe the disastrous results of neglected cases, but the task is an invidious one.

27. There can be no doubt that few patients are aware how much they can do for themselves. What the patient can do for himself, the forces he can set in motion are as yet unknown. We are inclined to believe that they are far greater than most imagine, and will undoubtedly be used more and more. **Mental therapeutics may be directed by the patient himself to calming the mind in excitement, by arousing feelings of joy, hope, faith, and love; by suggesting motives for exertion, by regular mental work, by diverting the thoughts from the malady**.

28. For your exercise this week concentrate on **Tennyson's** beautiful lines »Speak to Him, thou, for He hears, and spirit with spirit can meet, Closer is He than breathing, and nearer than hands and feet.« Then try to realize that when you do »Speak to Him« you are in touch with Omnipotence.

29. **This realization and recognition of this Omnipresent power will quickly destroy any and every form of sickness or suffering and substitute harmony and perfection**. Then remember there are those who seem to think that sickness and suffering are sent by God; if so, every physician, every surgeon and every Red Cross nurse is defying the will

Mental healing is what has taken place more and more since Charles Haanel wrote this chapter, but the best is still to come. For more of this kind, please listen to or read Gregg Braden's "The Lost Mode of Prayer", excerpts of which you will also find on Youtube. There is also an increasing amount of material becoming available from the Far East, where children display what we would call miraculous skills. These are signs of the new consciousness that is being born. Simply amazing!

Lord Alfred Tennyson (1809 – 1892)

of God and hospitals and sanitariums are places of rebellion instead of houses of mercy. Of course, this quickly reasons itself into an absurdity, but there are many who still cherish the idea.

30. Then let the thought rest on the fact that until recently **theology has been trying to teach an impossible Creator**, one who created beings capable of sinning, and then allowed them to be eternally punished for such sins. Of course the necessary outcome of such extraordinary ignorance was to create fear instead of love, and so, after two thousand years of this kind of propaganda, Theology is now busily engaged in apologizing for Christendom.

31. You will then more readily appreciate the Ideal Man, the Man made in the image and likeness of God, and you will more readily appreciate the all-originating Mind that forms, upholds, sustains, originates, and creates all there is. »*All are but parts of one stupendous whole, Whose body nature is, and God the soul.*« **Opportunity follows perception, action follows inspiration, growth follows knowledge, eminence follows progress.** Always the spiritual first, then the transformation into the infinite and illimitable possibilities of achievement.

"Though an inheritance of acres may be bequeathed, an inheritance of knowledge and wisdom cannot. The wealthy man may pay others for doing his work for him, but it is impossible to get his thinking done for him by another or to purchase any kind of self-culture."
— S. SMILES

211. *How may sickness be eliminated?*
By placing ourselves in harmony with
Natural Law which is omnipotent.

212. *What is the process?*
A realization that man is a spiritual being and
that this spirit must necessarily be perfect.

213. *What is the result?*
A conscious recognition of this perfection –
first intellectually, then emotionally – brings
about a manifestation of this perfection.

214. *Why is this so?*
Because thought is spiritual and therefore creative and
correlates with its object and brings it into manifestation.

215. *What Natural Law is brought into operation?*
The Law of Vibration.

216. *Why does this govern?*
Because a higher rate of vibration governs, modifies,
controls, changes, or destroys a lower rate of vibration.

217. *Is this system of mental therapeutics generally recognized?*
Yes, there are literally millions of people in this
country (the USA, Ed.), who make use of it in one form
or another (and obviously many more world-wide).

218. *What is the result of this system of thought?*
For the first time in the world's history every man's highest
reasoning faculty can be satisfied by a demonstrable
truth which is now fast flooding the world.

219. *Is this system applicable to other forms of supply?*
It will meet every human requirement or necessity.

220. *Is this system scientific or religious?*
Both. True science and true religion are twin sisters,
where one goes, the other necessarily follows.

SERVING MANKIND WITH A MONEY CONSCIOUSNESS

In the part which I have the honour to transmit herewith you will find that money weaves itself into the entire fabric of our very existence; that **the law of success is service**; that we get what we give, and for this reason we should consider it a great privilege to be able to give.

We have found that thought is the creative activity behind every constructive enterprise. We can therefore give nothing of more practical value than our thought.

Creative thought requires attention, and the power of attention is, as we have found, the weapon of the Super-man. **Attention develops concentration, and concentration develops Spiritual Power, and Spiritual Power is the mightiest force in existence.**

This is the science which embraces all sciences. It is the art which, above all arts, is relevant to human life. In the mastery of this science and this art there is opportunity for unending progression. Perfection in this is not acquired in six days, nor in six weeks, nor in six months. It is the labour of life. Not to go forward is to go backward.

It is inevitable that the entertainment of positive, constructive and unselfish thoughts should have a far-reaching effect for good. Compensation is the key-note of the Universe. Nature is constantly seeking to strike an equilibrium. Where something is sent out something must be received; else there should be a vacuum formed. By observance of this rule you cannot fail to profit in such measure as to amply justify your effort along this line.

SERVING MANKIND WITH A MONEY CONSCIOUSNESS

1. The money consciousness is an **attitude of mind**; it is the open door to the arteries of commerce. It is the receptive attitude. Desire is the attractive force which sets the current in motion and fear is the great obstacle by which the current is stopped or completely reversed, turned away from us.

2. **Fear is just the opposite from money consciousness**; it is poverty consciousness, and as the law is unchangeable we get exactly what we give; if we fear we get what we feared. Money

This expands your "Sphere of Availability". Mental powers increase through use, so what was once way out of reach has now become commonplace for us. Small successes lead to large successes!

You can make a money magnet of yourself, but to do so you must first consider how you can make money for other people.

weaves itself into the entire fabric of our very existence; it engages the best thought of the best minds.

3. We make money by making friends, and we enlarge our circle of friends by making money for them, by helping them, by being of service to them. The first law of success then is service, and this in turn is built on integrity and justice. The man who at least is not fair in his intention is simply ignorant; he has missed the fundamental law of all exchange; he is impossible; he will lose surely and certainly; he may not know it; he may think he is winning, but he is doomed to certain defeat. He cannot cheat the Infinite. The law of compensation will demand of him an eye for an eye and a tooth for a tooth.

4. The forces of life are volatile; they are composed of our thoughts and ideals and these in turn are moulded into form; our problem is to keep an open mind, to constantly reach out for the new, to recognize opportunity, to be interested in the race rather than the goal, for the pleasure is in the pursuit rather than the possession.

5. You can make a money magnet of yourself, but to do so you must first consider how you can make money for other people. If you have the necessary insight to perceive and utilize opportunities and favourable conditions and recognize values, you can put yourself in position to take advantage of them, but **your greatest success will come as you are enabled to assist others**. **What benefits one must benefit all**.

6. A generous thought is filled with strength and vitality, a selfish thought contains the germs of dissolution; it will disintegrate and pass away. Great financiers like Morgan, Rockefeller, Carnegie, and others are simply channels for the distribution of wealth; **enormous amounts come and go**, but it would be as dangerous to stop the outgo as the income; both ends must remain open; and so our greatest success

"Assisting others" is most likely the "hardest nut" to crack, because conventional thinking goes as follows: "How am I to make money for others if I don't have money myself? This is impossible!" However, now, after 22 weeks of studying, you are versed in the workings of the inner world. You know how things come into manifestation. You also know that you can rely on the right people at being the right places, doing the right things at the right time. You know that your Conscious Mind can't possibly fathom the workings of the Universal, but it knows that all is subject to law.

With this in mind, the services or products (the Ideal!) are being born in your mind, in the Silence, concentrating on the outcome as an already established fact. The rest will work itself out according to plan with you as a person of courage and determination. This is how you serve others and make money for them – and they for you!

It is clear by now that just thinking about wealth or happiness is not getting you anywhere. Thought has to be converted into tangible values, and those tangible values are the result of action. But knowing that the end result will have had a corresponding sponsoring thought (cause), it will be easy for you to kick into action, "stand erect and work miracles".

will come as we recognize that it is just as essential to give as to get.

7. If we recognize the omnipotent power that is the source of all supply we will adjust our consciousness to this supply in such a way that it will constantly attract all that is necessary to itself, and **we shall find that the more we give the more we get**. Giving in this sense implies **service**. The banker gives his money, the merchant gives his goods, the author gives his thought, the workman gives his skill; all have something to give, but the more they can give, the more they get, and the more they get the more they are enabled to give.

8. The financier gets much because he gives much; he thinks; he is seldom a man that lets anyone else do his thinking for him; he wants to know how results are to be secured; you must show him; when you can do this he will furnish the means by which hundreds or thousands may profit, and in proportion as they are successful will he be successful. Morgan, Rockefeller, Carnegie and others did not get rich because they lost money for other people; on the contrary, it is because they made money for other people that they became the wealthiest men in the wealthiest country on the globe.

9. **The average person is entirely innocent of any deep thinking**; he accepts the ideas of others, and repeats them, in very much the same way as a parrot. This is readily seen when we understand the method which is used to form public opinion, and **this docile attitude on the part of a large majority who seem perfectly willing to let a few persons do all their thinking for them is what enables a few men in a great many countries to usurp all the avenues of power and hold the millions in subjection**. Creative thinking requires attention.

In order to "refuse to concentrate on anything except the things you desire", you have to "reverse the evidence of our senses" and keep holding onto your ideal in the Silence, until it has grown roots and built a strong foundation for any kind of action; until it can no longer be destroyed by residual doubt or the criticism of other people. This is the hard mental labour Charles Haanel is talking about.

10. The power of attention is called concentration; this power is directed by the will; for this reason **we must refuse to concentrate or think of anything except the things we desire**. Many are constantly concentrating upon sorrow, loss and discord of every kind; as thought is creative it necessarily follows that this concentration inevitable leads to more loss, more sorrow and more discord. How could it be otherwise?

On the other hand, when we meet with success, gain, or any other desirable condition, we naturally concentrate upon the effects of these things and thereby create more, and so it follows that **much leads to more**.

11. How an understanding of this principle can be utilized in the business world is well told by an associate of mine:

12. »Spirit, whatever else it may or may not be, must be considered as the Essence of Consciousness, the Substance of Mind, the reality underlying Thought. And as all ideas are phases of the activity of Consciousness, Mind or Thought, it follows that in Spirit, and in it alone, is to be found the Ultimate Fact, the Real Thing, or Idea.«

13. This being admitted, does it not seem reasonable to hold that a true understanding of Spirit, and its laws of manifestation, would be about the most »practical« thing that a »practical« person can hope to find? Does it not seem certain that if the »practical« men of the world could but realize this fact, they would »fall all over themselves« in getting to the place in which they might obtain such knowledge of spiritual things and laws? These men are not fools; they need only to grasp this fundamental fact in order to move in the direction of that which is the essence of all achievement.

14. Let me give you a concrete example. I know a man in Chicago whom I had always considered to be quite materialistic. He had made several successes in life; and also several failures. The last time I had a talk with him he was practically »down and out,« as compared with his former business condition. It looked as if he had indeed reached »the end of his rope,« for he was well advanced into the stage of middle-age, and new ideas came more slowly, and less frequently to him than in former years.

15. He said to me, in substance: »I know that all things that ‚work out‘ in business are the result of Thought; any fool knows that. Just now, I seem to be short on thoughts and good ideas. But, if this ‚All-Mind‘ teaching is correct, it should be possible for the individual to attain a ‚direct connection‘ with Infinite Mind; and in Infinite Mind there must be the possibility of all kinds of good ideas which a man of my courage and

253

This is an example of an open and therefore receptive mind. The person may not have understood all about it, but he was willing enough to investigate rather than letting programming and prejudice get in his way. This kind of openness to opportunity is what characterizes any successful business-person.

experience could put to practical use in the business world, and make a big success thereof. It looks good to me; and I am going to look into it.«

16. This was several years ago. The other day I heard of this man again. Talking to a friend, I said: »What has come of our old friend X? Has he ever gotten on his feet again?« The friend looked at me in amazement. »Why,« said he, »don't you know about X's great success? He is the Big Man in the ,_ _ _ _ _ Company' (naming a concern which has mad a phenomenal success during the last eighteen months and is now well known, by reason of its advertisements, from one end of the country to another, and also abroad). He is the man who supplied the BIG IDEA for that concern. Why, he is about a half-million to the good and is moving rapidly toward the million mark; all in the space of eighteen months.« I had not connected this man with the enterprise mentioned; although I knew of the wonderful success of the company in question. Investigation has shown that the story is true, and that the above stated facts are not exaggerated in the slightest.

17. Now, what do you think of that? To me, it means that this man actually made the »direct connection« with Infinite Mind — Spirit — and, having found it, he set it to work for him. He »used it in his business.«

18. Does this sound sacrilegious or blasphemous? I hope not; I do not mean it to be so. Take away the implication of Personality, or Magnified Human Nature, from the conception of the »The Infinite,« and you have left the conception of an Infinite Presence-Power, the Quintessence of which is Consciousness — in fact, at the last, Spirit. As this man, also, at the last, must be considered as a manifestation of Spirit; there is nothing sacrilegious in the idea that he, being Spirit, should so harmonize himself with his Origin and Source that he would be able to manifest at least a minor degree of its Power. All of us do this, more or less, when we use our minds in the direction of Creative Thought. This man did more, he went about it in an intensely »practical« manner.

19. I have not consulted him about his method of procedure, though I intend doing so at the first opportunity, but, he not

Man is not a body with a spirit, but a spirit with a body. For this reason his desires are incapable of any permanent satisfaction in anything not spiritual.

only drew upon the Infinite Supply for the ideas which he needed (and which formed the seed of his success), but that he also used the Creative Power of Thought in building up for himself an Idealistic Pattern of that which he hoped to manifest in material form, adding thereto, changing, improving its detail from time to time — proceeding from the general outline to the finished detail. I judge this to be the facts of the case, not alone from my recollection of the conversation a few years ago, but also because I have found the same thing to be true in the cases of other prominent men who have made similar manifestation of Creative Thought.

20. Those who may shrink from this idea of employing the Infinite Power to aid one in his work in the material world, should remember that if the Infinite objected in the least to such a procedure the thing could never happen. **The Infinite is quite able to take care of Itself.**

21. »Spirituality« is quite »practical,« very »practical,« intensely »practical.« It teaches that Spirit is the Real Thing, the Whole Thing, and that Matter is but plastic stuff, which Spirit is able to create, mould, manipulate, and fashion to its will. Spirituality is the most »practical« thing in the world — the only really and absolutely »practical« thing that there is!

22. This week concentrate on the fact that man is not a body with a spirit, but a spirit with a body, and that it is for this reason that his **desires are incapable of any permanent satisfaction in anything not spiritual**. Money is therefore of no value except to bring about the conditions which we desire, and these conditions are necessarily harmonious. Harmonious conditions necessitate sufficient supply, so that if there appears to be any lack, we should realize that **the**

Remember that it is a state of consciousness that you are after, namely happiness and harmony. All financial or material things are just tools, or means to an end, but not the end itself. Never let this slip your mind!

255

idea or soul of money is service, and as this thought takes form, channels of supply will be opened, and you will have the satisfaction of knowing that spiritual methods are entirely practical.

"We have discovered that premeditated, orderly thinking for a purpose matures that purpose into fixed form, so that we may be absolutely sure of the result of our dynamic experiment."
— FRANCIS LARIMER WARNER

PART TWENTY-THREE — QUESTIONS AND ANSWERS

221. *What is the first law of success?*
Service.

222. *How may we be of the most service?*
Have an open mind; be interested in the race rather
than the goal, in the pursuit rather than possession.

223. *What is the result of a selfish thought?*
It contains the germs of dissolution.

224. *How will our greatest success be achieved?*
By a recognition of the fact that it is just
as essential to give as to receive.

225. *Why do financiers frequently meet with great success?*
Because they do their own thinking.

226. *Why do the great majority in every country remain
the docile and apparently willing tools of the few?*
Because they let the few do all their thinking for them.

227. *What is the effect of concentrating upon sorrow and loss?*
More sorrow and more loss.

228. *What is the effect of concentrating upon gain?*
More gain.

229. *Is this principle used in the business world?*
It is the only principle which is ever used, or ever can
be used; there is no other principle. The fact that it may
be used unconsciously does not alter the situation.

230. *What is the practical application of this principle?*
The fact that success is an effect, not a cause, and if we
wish to secure the effect we must ascertain the cause,
or idea or thought by which the effect is created.

24

THE TRUTH SHALL SET YOU FREE

Enclosed you will find Part Twenty-four, your final lesson of this course.

If you have practiced each of the exercises a few minutes every day, as suggested, you will have found that **xou can get out of life exactly what you wish by first putting into life that which you wish**, and you will probably agree with the student who said: »The thought is almost overwhelming, so vast, so available, so definite, so reasonable and so usable.«

The fruit of this knowledge is, as it were, a gift of the Gods; it is the »truth« that makes men free, not only free from every lack and limitation, but free from sorrow, worry and care, and, is it not wonderful to realize that this law is no respecter of persons, that it makes no difference what your habit of thought may be, the way has been prepared.

If you are inclined to be religious, the greatest religious teacher the world has ever known made the way so plain that all may follow. If your mental bias is toward physical science, the law will operate with mathematical certainty. If you are inclined to be philosophical, Plato or Emerson may be your teacher, but in either case, you may reach degrees of power to which it is impossible to assign any limit.

An understanding of this principle, I believe, is the secret for which the ancient Alchemists vainly sought, because it explains how **gold in the mind may be transmuted into gold in the heart and in the hand**.

THE TRUTH SHALL SET YOU FREE

1. When the scientists first put the Sun in the centre of the Solar System and sent the Earth spinning around it, there was immense surprise and consternation. The whole idea was self-evidently false; nothing was more certain than the movement of the Sun across the sky, and anyone could see it descend behind the western hills and sink into the sea; scholars raged and scientists rejected the idea as absurd, yet the evidence has finally carried conviction in the minds of all.

2. We speak of a bell as a »sounding body,« yet we know that all the bell can do is to produce vibrations in the air. When these vibrations come at the rate of sixteen per second, they cause a sound to be heard in the mind. It is also possible for the mind to hear vibrations up to the rate of 38,000 vibrations per second. When the number increases beyond this, all is silence again; so that we know that **the sound is not in the bell, it is in our own mind**.

3. We speak and even think of the Sun as »giving light.« Yet we know it is simply giving forth energy which produces vibrations in the ether at the rate of four hundred trillion a second, causing what are termed light waves, so that we know that we call light is simply a form of energy and that the only light there is, is **the sensation caused in the mind** by the motion of the waves. When the number increases, the light changes in colour, each change in colour being caused by shorter and more rapid vibrations; so that although we speak of the rose as being red, the grass as being green, or the sky as being blue, we know that the colours exist only in our minds, and are the sensations experienced by us as the result of the vibrations of light waves. When the vibrations are reduced below four hundred trillion a second, they no longer affect us as light, but we experience the sensation of heat. It is evident, therefore, that we cannot depend upon the evidence of the senses for our information concerning the realities of things; if we did we should believe that the sun moved, that the world was flat instead of round, that the stars were bits of light instead of vast suns.

This is yet another proof that reality is not created outside of us, but that it is us and our ability to perceive and interpret the various forms of vibration that is creating what we call our life, or our reality.

4. The whole range then of the theory and practice of any system of metaphysics consists in knowing the Truth concerning yourself and the world in which you live; in knowing that

Disease and lack are simply mental conditions
in which the person fails to perceive the Truth;
as soon as the error is removed, the condition is removed.

If you desire to help someone,
the correct method is to have the intention of helping them,
as this puts you in mental touch with the person.

A reference to John 8:32. Out of curiosity, if you continue reading John 8 and 9, you will find a perfect example of two parties talking past each other – transmitter and receiver clearly not being on the same wavelength. Here too, the Hermetic Principles came into application, because the Jews didn't understand what Jesus was saying. Although he spoke the Truth, he could have done better if he had adjusted them to the level of understanding of the Jews. This is just one of the many examples in history, where conflict arose from a lack of understanding. Let this be our lesson, and may we always find the right tone and level of communication for others to understand what we are trying to convey.

in order to express harmony, you must think harmony; in order to express health you must think health; and in order to express abundance you must think abundance; to do this you must reverse the evidence of the senses.

5. When you come to know that every form of disease, sickness, lack and limitation are **simply the result of wrong thinking**, you will have come to know »the Truth which shall make you free.« You will see how mountains may be removed. If these mountains consist only of doubt, fear, distrust or other forms of discouragement, they are none the less real, and they need not only to be removed but to be »cast into the sea.«

6. Your real work consists in convincing yourself of the truth of these statements. When you have succeeded in doing this you will have no difficulty in thinking the truth, and as has been shown, the truth contains a vital principle and will manifest itself.

7. Those who heal diseases by mental methods have come to know this Truth, they demonstrate it in their lives and the lives of others daily. They know that life, health and abundance are Omnipresent, filling all space, and they know that those who allow disease or lack of any kind to manifest, have as yet not come into an understanding of this great law.

8. As all conditions are thought creations and therefore entirely mental, disease and lack are simply mental conditions in which the person fails to perceive the Truth; as soon as the error is removed, the condition is removed.

9. The method for removing this error is to go into the Silence and know the Truth; as all mind is one mind, you can do this for yourself or anyone else. If you have learned to form mental images of the conditions desired, this will be the

easiest and quickest way to secure results; if not, results can be accomplished by argument, by the process of convincing yourself absolutely of the truth of your statement.

10. Remember, and this is one of the most difficult as well as most wonderful statements to grasp. Remember that no matter what the difficulty is, no matter where it is, no matter who is affected, **you have no patient but yourself**; you have nothing to do but to convince yourself of the truth which you desire to see manifested.

11. This is an exact scientific statement in accordance with every system of Metaphysics in existence, and no permanent results are ever secured in any other way.

12. **Every form of concentration, forming Mental Images, Argument, and Auto-Suggestion are all simply methods by which you are enabled to realize the Truth.**

13. If you desire to help someone, to destroy some form of lack, limitation or error, the correct method is not to think of the person whom you wish to help; **the intention to help them is entirely sufficient, as this puts you in mental touch with the person**. Then drive **out of your own mind** any belief of lack, limitation, disease, danger, difficulty or whatever the trouble might be. As soon as you have succeeded in doing this, the result will have been accomplished, and the person will be free.

14. But remember that thought is creative and consequently every time you allow your thought to rest on any inharmonious condition, you must realize that such conditions are apparent only, they have no reality, that **spirit is the only reality and it can never be less than perfect**.

15. All thought is a form of energy, a rate of vibration, but a thought of the Truth is the highest rate of vibration known, and consequently destroys every form of error in exactly the same way that light destroys darkness. **No form of error can**

Do you understand the significance of section 8 and 9? Whatever registers in your mind is the result of your consciousness. This is the place where any kind of healing takes place, knowing that the Individual is but a channel of expression for the Universal. As the Universal is based on structure, order, beauty, harmony and love, so should your own expression.

With your Conscious Mind you will never be able to fully grasp the workings of the Universal, but you can become a conscious outlet for its blessings.

Even though you don't understand (yet) how the sick become healed, the hungry fed, and the poor rich, these should be the images that you imprint on your Subconscious Mind, which is not only all substance, but also all intelligence!

No matter what the difficulty is, no matter where it is, no matter who is affected, you have no patient but yourself.

263

exist when the »Truth« appears, so that your entire mental work consists in coming into an understanding of the Truth. This will enable you to overcome every form of lack, limitation or disease of any kind.

16. We can get no understanding of the truth from the world without; **the world without is relative only**; Truth is absolute. We must therefore find it in the »world within.«

17. To train the mind to see Truth only is to express true conditions only, our ability to do this will be an indication as to the progress we are making.

18. The absolute truth is that the »I« is perfect and complete; **the real »I« is spiritual and can therefore never be less than perfect**; it can never have any lack, limitation, or disease. The flash of genius does not have origin in the molecular motion of the brain; it is inspired by the ego, the spiritual »I« which is one with the Universal Mind, and it is our ability to recognize this Unity which is the cause of all inspiration, all genius. These results are far reaching and have effect upon generations yet to come; they are the pillars of fire which mark the path that millions follow.

19. Truth is not the result of logical training or of experimentation, or even of observation; it is **the product of a developed consciousness**. Truth within a Caesar, manifests in a Caesar's deportment, in his life and his action; his influence upon social forms and progress. **Your life and your actions and your influence in the world will depend upon the degree of truth which you are enabled to perceive, for truth will not manifest in creeds, but in conduct**.

20. Truth manifests in character, and the character of a man, should be the interpretation of his religion, or what to him is truth, and this will in turn be evidenced in the character of his possession. If a man complains of the drift of his fortune he is just as unjust to himself as if he should deny rational truth, though it stand patent and irrefutable.

21. Our environment and the innumerable circumstances and accidents of our lives already exist in the subconscious personality which attracts to itself the mental and physical material which is congenial to its nature. Thus our future

And why? Because there is only one Consciousness, which cannot be less than perfect. Our conscious unity with the Universal Mind is what brings about all the desired mental, physical and emotional states. and manifestations.

No form of error can exist when the »Truth« appears, so that your entire mental work consists in coming into an understanding of the Truth.

being determined from our present, and if there should be apparent injustice in any feature or phase of our personal life, we must look within for the cause, try to discover the mental fact which is responsible for the outward manifestation.

22. It is this truth which makes you »free« and it is the conscious knowledge of this truth which will enable you to overcome every difficulty.

23. The conditions with which you meet in the world without are invariably the result of the conditions obtaining in the world within, therefore it follows with scientific accuracy that **by holding the perfect ideal in mind you can bring about ideal conditions in your environment.**

24. If you see only the incomplete, the imperfect, the relative, the limited, these conditions will manifest in your life; but if you train your mind to see and realize the spiritual ego, the »I« which is forever perfect and complete, harmonious, wholesome, and healthful conditions only will be manifested.

25. As thought is creative, and the truth is the highest and most perfect thought which anyone can think, it is self-evident that **to think the truth is to create that which is true** and it is again evident that when truth comes into being that which is false must cease to be.

26. The Universal Mind is the totality of all mind which is in existence. Spirit is mind, because spirit is intelligent. The words are, therefore, synonymous.

27. The difficulty with which you have to contend is to realize that mind is not individual. It is omnipresent. It exists everywhere. In other words, there is no place where it is not. It is, therefore, universal.

28. Men have, heretofore, generally used the word »God« to indicate this universal, creative principle, but the word »God«

does not convey the right meaning. Most people understand this word to mean something outside of themselves; while exactly the contrary is the fact. **It is our very life**. Without it we would be dead. We would cease to exist. The minute the spirit leaves the body, we are as nothing. Therefore, spirit is really, all there is of us.

29. Now, the only activity which the spirit possesses is the power to think. Therefore, **thought must be creative, because spirit is creative**. This creative power is impersonal and your ability to think is your ability to control it and make use of it for the benefit of yourself and others.

30. When the truth of this statement is realized, understood, and appreciated, you will have come into possession of the **Master Key**, but remember that only those who are **wise enough to understand**, **broad enough to weigh the evidence, firm enough to follow their own judgment**, and **strong enough to make the sacrifice exacted**, may enter and partake.

31. This week, try to realize that this is truly a wonderful world in which we live; that you are a wonderful being; that many are awakening to a knowledge of the Truth, and as fast as they awake and come into a knowledge of the »things which have been prepared for them« they, too, realize that »Eye hath not seen, nor ear heard, neither hath it entered into the heart of man,« the splendours which exist for those who find themselves in the Promised Land. They have crossed the river of judgment and have arrived at the point of discrimination between the true and the false, and have found that all they ever willed or dreamed, was but a faint concept of a dazzling reality.

*Temples have their sacred images, and
we see what influence they have always
had over a great part of mankind; but,
in truth, the ideas and images in men's
minds are the invisible powers that
constantly govern them; and to these they
all pay universally a ready submission.*
— JONATHAN EDWARDS

267

231. *Upon what principle does the theory and practice of every system of Metaphysics in existence depend?*
Upon a knowledge of the »Truth« concerning yourself and the world in which you life.

232. *What is the »Truth« concerning yourself?*
The real »I« or ego is spiritual and can therefore never be less than perfect.

233. *What is the method of destroying any form of error?*
To absolutely convince yourself of the »Truth« concerning the condition which you wish to see manifested.

234. *Can we do this for others?*
The Universal Mind in which »we live and move and have our being« is one and indivisible, it is therefore just as possible to help others as to help ourselves.

235. *What is the Universal Mind?*
The totality of all mind in existence.

236. *Where is the Universal Mind?*
The Universal Mind is omnipresent, it exists everywhere. There is no place where it is not. It is therefore within us. It is »The World within.« It is our spirit, our life.

237. *What is the nature of the Universal Mind?*
It is spiritual and consequently creative. It seeks to express itself in form.

238. *How may we act on the Universal Mind?*
Our ability to think is our ability to act on the Universal Mind and bring it into manifestation for the benefit of ourselves or others.

239. *What is meant by thinking?*
Clear, decisive, calm, deliberate, sustained thought with a definite end in view.

240. *What will be the result?*

You will also be able to say, »It is not I that doeth the works, but the »Father« that dwelleth within me, He doeth the works.« You will come to know that the »Father« is the Universal Mind and that He does really and truly dwell within you, in other words, you will come to know that the wonderful promises made in the Bible are fact, not fiction, and can be demonstrated by anyone having sufficient understanding.

"Thought means life, since those who do not think do not live in any high or real sense. Thinking makes the man."
— A. B. ALCOTT

THE VISUAL MASTER KEY™

A world-first: The Master Key System on a cylindrical 360 degrees panorama for lateral thinking, accelerated learning and the removal of blockages – only €29,00.

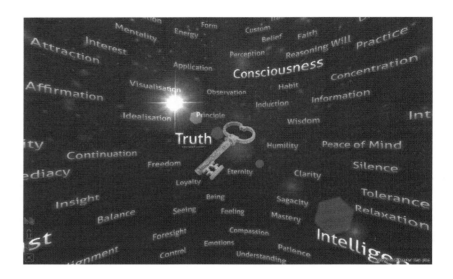

It has always been my goal to simplify the Master Key System, so that students finish the course and reap the greatest benefit. It soon became apparent that this wouldn't be in writing another book, but in a completely different approach to learning.

Following some experimentation, I extracted the most important keywords from the Master Key System and added a few of my own. There are currently nearly 200 words on this panorama, each one with an explanation and links to its mention in the book.

The Visual Master Key is a very powerful tool that displays the entire Creative Process in a seamless fashion – this has never been done before in such a way! The application can be used both in an alert and awake ("beta") as well as a relaxed ("alpha") state of mind. You can focus and concentrate on particular words or clusters, or zoom out and glance over the arrangement of words in a meditative fashion, without any conscious effort.

The Visual Master Key is an online Flash application and costs only **€29,00** (app. US$41.00). It can be ordered and enjoyed at www.MasterKeySystem.tv.

THE MASTER KEY BRAINCHARGER WORKBOOK

Train your brain and test your knowledge with this premium workbook for only $15.95, the perfect companion of your Master Key System studies.

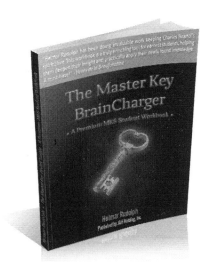

The Master Key BrainCharger Premium Workbook was derived from the online 24-week study service. It was completely rewritten and amended for this print version.

Each of the 24 chapters features introductory notes, as well as insight into the exercises.

The body of the workbook has a number of static multiple-choice questions that allow the student to monitor the progress made over the weeks.

As the chapters go by, the free-text questions are becoming increasingly difficult and demanding, testing the student real hard. The results, however, are worth the effort.

A selection of book and video recommendations are rounding off this valuable study companion, while there is still plenty of room for personal notes. All in all a great workbook for the serious Master Key System student.

The Master Key BrainCharger costs **$15.95** and can be ordered straight from my website or at Amazon.com.

THE MASTER KEY STUDY SERVICE

Enrol in this unique email-based study service containing two emails per week and a video for each of the 24 chapters. Only €59.00.

Studying the Master Key System is no easy feat. If you stick to the schedule, it will keep you busy for at least half a year. In order to ease your way, I created a study service which informs and motivates you for the entire duration of the course.

Starting on a Sunday, you will receive an email with an introduction to the chapter, while on Wednesday you will be receiving another email with further insights and tips.

Each chapter contains access to a video of between 15 and 40 minutes length where I explain they key words and concepts of the Master Key System.

This service will help you finish your studies and get the most out of this amazing teaching.

The Master Key System Study Service costs **€59.00** and can be ordered on www.masterkeysystem.tv.

CLOUDWALK

The first ever musical journey through the Master Key System. 72 minutes of pure bliss, inspiration and mental creativity. Only $18.00.

For a long time it's been my dream to convey the contents of the Master Key System using music as a medium, because it transcends all language barriers. At the same time it bypasses the conscious mind and works its magic on a different level of creation.

When I found the Latvian musician and composer Gulan, I immediately knew that my search had come to an end. As fate wanted it, Gulan welcomed the idea with open arms, and this CD saw the light of day. It is a unique compilation of tracks that I gathered from several of his albums, arranging them in such a way that a journey representing your path of enlightenment would emerge.

"Cloudwalk" takes you back to the origins of creation, then gently alerts you to the infinite possibilities, which are gradually taking shape. After the first phase of enlightenment, you will be taken into a deep meditative phase, from which you awaken refreshed and renewed. You will feel motivated and determined, courageous and bold, while the final track ends in a beautiful orchestral crescendo, a culmination of your knowledge, insight and practical application.

This is a true gem of a CD, which is available for only **$18.00** at Amazon.com.

VALUABLE TIPS

1. Start off affirming to yourself that you are good enough and that you deserve only the best in life.
2. Acknowledge that it's a process that will take time, but that will be worth every effort made.
3. Write down your goals on paper, irrespective of how unattainable they may appear at first.
4. Create a Vision-Board with magazine clippings of the things you desire or that represent states you would like to attain.
5. If you spend a lot of time on the computer, use the desktop background as a Vision-Board or get some specialised software to do that. The same applies to the screensaver.
6. Every day before going to bed, give thanks for all the wonderful things that happened that day. Develop an attitude of gratitude.
7. Every morning, before you get up, spend some thoughts on what you will accomplish this day.
8. While in the bathroom, fire yourself up, i.e. jump up and down on the spot, while looking yourself in the eye.
9. Take cold showers, preferably outside, for the negative ions will result in you feeling really good.
10. Make good use of fridge magnets to pin positive words or phrases on the door.
11. Understand that the Creative Process is unlike stuff that already exists. It is the calling into existence of something that's not there yet. It takes time for your Mind to get a handle on it.
12. Become aware of the small things in life. They can be observed pretty much everywhere. All it takes is some attention of yours.
13. Make sure your nutritional diet is in line with the goals you have set for yourself. In order to accomplish great things, you will need a lot of good food, not only for your thinking processes, but for physical work, too.
14. Mingle with people who have accomplished that which you still wish to. Try to stay away from people who are negative or overly critical. If that fails, spend as much time in nature as possible.
15. Remember that if someone else has accomplished something, you can accomplish it, too. Find out for yourself what you really love to do. Don't set any limits on yourself.

16. Reward yourself regularly for progress made.
17. Keep in mind that life is meant to be fun and not a drudge.
18. Keep reminding yourself that nowhere is written what you have to think. You can always change your thoughts. You are the Master of your destiny.
19. Make a habit of reading quality books, i.e. autobiographies of great and successful people.
20. If possible, create a daily routine that includes at least 1.5 hours for your MKS studies. You will need that much time. You are welcome to split reading and doing the exercise.
21. Laugh as often as you can. It is healthy and feels good. Pull faces until you cannot but laugh. It's also a great way to exercise your facial muscles, making you look younger and more radiant.
22. Do unusual things, for they disrupt your standard thinking patterns and force you to look at things with different eyes.
23. When going to work, driving down a well-known road or being a place that you know well, look at the setup with completely different eyes, i.e. when on a West-facing beach, place it in another country and make it face North. Then notice how its look and feel changes. Do this regularly.
24. Remind yourself that life is not only about money, but if you want more money, you will need to be appreciative of it. Review your stance towards money on a regular basis.
25. Visit nice places often. Hotel bars and restaurants are perfect for this. There you can have tea and soak up the elegant atmosphere.
26. When paying bills, do so with joy and gratitude. Someone else will get your money with really good vibes attached to it.
27. If you feel lonely in your studies, form a group with other students, even if it's just one other person.
28. Remind yourself as often as you can that your real "I" is perfect.
29. Spend as much time in nature as you can.
30. Drink good clean water. If necessary, get a water filter.
31. Make use of music based on the ancient Solfeggio scale.
32. Understand that practice makes perfect. "Fake it 'til you make it", and have lots of fun while doing it!
33. Finally, why not use this wonderful affirmation given to Dr. John Demartini, a renowned inspirational speaker, when he was a young boy: "I am a genius, and I apply my wisdom."

NOTES

NOTES

NOTES

NOTES

23772811R00151

Made in the USA
Lexington, KY
23 June 2013